Caregiving

Journey to a New Horizon

Glen A. Hinshaw

E. Laird Landon Jr., PhD

Caregiving: Journey to a New Horizon

Published by Glen A. Hinshaw and E. Laird Landon Jr., PhD
Cover photo by Mark A. Hunzaker
Cover design by Glen A. Hinshaw
Editor: Hedda Marg

ISBN: 9798646127786

Caregiving, Alzheimer's, Dementia, Parkinson's, Aging, Grief, Support Group,

Available from Amazon in paperback or as a Kindle eBook.
On Facebook search for us: 'Caregiver Journey' or 'Caregiver Support'
Email us: CaregiverSupport@icloud.com.

"The powerful and gut-wrenching stories shared in 'Caregiving, Journey to a New Horizon' put you right in the middle of what a caregiving support group must be like, where raw struggles are brought to the surface, difficult emotions are openly and honestly shared, and people are empowered to speak what they feel. This book is a must-read for anyone who feels trapped and overwhelmed in their caregiving role and needs a breath of fresh air as it will give you the tools you need for the journey ahead."
Alan J. Gibson J. D. M. Div

"This book is worthwhile for anyone on the caregiver journey. Seniors who are not caregivers would benefit from reading this book to mentally prepare for the future."
Robert K. Scott PhD

"This is not just a good read; it is a roadmap for all of us. I have been caring for my wife who has a neurological disease for several years. I was struggling and feeling like I was at the end of my rope. It is a blessing to be able to follow a guide that shows my past mistakes and plan for events and issues in the future for both of us. This is a very personal book that gave me understanding of my emotions and inner being,"
Dr Gary D. Lindberg, DPE

"This book should be read by any potential or current caregiver as well as by their families and friends. The stories are told, not by academics but by ordinary people who have lived the extraordinary journey of being a caregiver. The book gives a comprehensive and emotional look at each stage of the caregiver's journey and provides insights into how to deal with the inevitable loss of their loved one with courage and with hope."
Mark Smith, veteran caregiver

"What an amazing book. I am totally blown away by the honesty and the effective way you have divided caregiving phases into chapters. Well done!"

Cliff Martin, veteran caregiver

Dedication

We dedicate this book to all the caregivers who have shared their journeys with us. We are grateful for what each of you has taught us. We further dedicate the book to all family caregivers who sacrifice of themselves to care for another. We dedicate this book to health care professionals who look after caregivers and their loved ones.

Acknowledgments

Thank you to the following contributors:

LaMoine Brown, Richard Burge, Beverly Dwire, Kevin Harvey, Esther Hinshaw. Eleanor Mullendore, BJ Myers, Kathy Nelson, Jennifer Rohweder, Jerilyn Sheldon, Bettye Sinner, Ronda Steenburgen, Robert Stine, Frank Tanner, Sandra Wagnon, Sheri Weaver.

Thank you to following reviewers:

Jane Barton, Cath Duncan, Ralph Fry, Gary Lindberg, Carol Friedrich, Cliff Martin, Floyd Penna, Becky Powers, Robert K. Scott. and Mark Smith. We also thank Hedda Marg for editing. Special thanks to Lois Jump for her assistance.

Preface

A lonely caregiver walks his dog on a road that has many hills as it winds upward through a forest. Ultimately the road reaches the summit that reveals a new horizon with new panoramas on the other side. In this metaphor I (Glen), walked that caregiver road for 36 years. The early years of my journey were lonely and scary. I felt the panic of being alone, lost, and confused. I sought a counselor who walked alongside of me pointing things out in the forest that I hadn´t seen because of all those trees.

Twenty-five years later Laird joined me along that road and we discovered that we had a lot in common. We wanted to do everything possible to help our wives and now we can look back at our caregiving years with no regrets. We learned everything we could about dementia. We learned how to be better caregivers for them and to take care of ourselves as well. We learned about resources to help us give the best care we could give at home. We learned that we had more resilience and inner strength than we realized.

We grieved the slow loss of our wives over an extremely long time. We accepted the fact that we had little control over our circumstances. It took a while to learn patience, but we did. We learned to cherish the lucid moments and the times when we could make a difference. The hardest thing to accept was that our wives had diseases for which there is no cure and they would slowly die and there was nothing we could do to slow or stop the progression.

Along the way other struggling caregivers joined us. Because we were farther down the road, they asked questions. We found ourselves having coffee while coaching them along their journeys. They just needed to talk to someone who understood how they felt. We listened, withheld judgment, and resisted the temptation to give advice.

Our local Area Agency on Aging (AAA) was responsive to what we were doing and invited us to facilitate a floundering support group in the same way we coached individuals. The caregivers were caring for loved ones with diseases such as Alzheimer's, Parkinson's, multiple sclerosis (MS), stroke, brain injury, or another disability. It didn't matter whether they were caring for a parent, spouse, child or friend.

The caregivers in our group were caring for loved ones in different stages of disease and they lifted each other up by sharing their emotions, confident of being in a safe place. They shared how they coped and they gleaned from each other ideas that made them better caregivers as well as showing them how to take good care of themselves. We cried and laughed together as we shared our journeys. These caregivers were creative problem solvers who shared how they dealt with daily challenges - such as inappropriate behaviors that made them angry. All found encouragement, understanding, and comfort as their common experiences bonded them together.

We wrote this book to share what we have learned from our own experiences and those of other caregivers. We hope caregivers and professionals who work with patients and families with long-term terminal illnesses will find it useful.

Please take good care of yourself.

Glen A. Hinshaw and E. Laird Landon Jr., PhD

Foreword

In April of 2017, I traveled to the Western Slope of Colorado to present several educational programs at a caregiving conference. While at the conference, I was blessed to meet Glen and Laird. Over the course of several days, they graciously shared their stories of caregiving that touched my heart and soul. This book is a compilation of those stories and many more—stories that will inform, inspire, challenge, encourage, empower, comfort, and validate you.

Having served as a family caregiver numerous times beginning at the age of 15, I greatly appreciate "the why" of this book. Glen and Laird wrote this book in the hope of helping caregivers (family and professional) who are knee-deep in the trenches of caregiving. Wherever you are in the journey and whatever you are feeling, it's reassuring to know that other people have traveled a similar path. Glen and Laird—along with the other caregivers highlighted in the book— have been there and done that! They get it. Thus, you will resonate with the stories contained in ***Caregiving: Journey to a New Horizon.***

Answering the call to care for a family member, friend, or patient is one of the highest callings in life - a sacred calling in many ways. However, caring for another person may prove to be one of the hardest things we ever do. It often takes everything we must give—and then some! Caregiving challenges us physically, emotionally, spiritually, financially, and psychosocially. So it's no wonder there are moments when we doubt our ability (or willingness) to fulfill this role.

Because caregiving is challenging, I greatly appreciate the stories shared in this book. The caregivers are real, raw, and authentic when telling their respective tales. The reality of caring is not meant to frighten you. Instead, by realistically portraying the day-to-day issues, the authors hope to prepare you for the inevitable twists and turns along the way. Forewarned is forearmed. Based on my personal and professional experience as a caregiver, we are better served to be proactive rather than reactive. The stories of Glen and Laird, and the other caregivers will help you prepare to care.

In the future, we will undoubtedly witness advances in medical technology, disease prevention, and pharmacology that will impact the prevalence and the severity of various diseases. However, serving as a caregiver will remain a significant challenge for all who answer the call. Hence, ***Caregiving; Journey to a New Horizon*** will prove to be a timeless resource for caregivers, because it addresses what it ***feels*** like to be a caregiver. So, savor the book you hold in your hands. Cherish the poignant stories of other caregivers. Consider the hard-earned wisdom contained between the front and back covers of this book. Then trust that your journey of caregiving will also lead to new a horizon - one step at a time. May it be so! Blessings to you and yours.

Jane W. Barton, MTS, MASM, CSA
Cardinal, LLC
Speaker, Writer, Listener
Author of ***Caregiving for the GENIUS***

Table of Contents

Chapter 5

Advocate: I advise and protect

Chapter 6

Grieve: I remember and adjust to a new life

Introduction

People have been caregivers for thousands of years. For most of its existence America was an agrarian society. More people lived in rural areas than in cities until 1920. Before then, caregiving was done by family and most deaths came relatively quickly, due to accidents, infection, sickness, and old age. Health care was done at home using home remedies.

It was not uncommon for three generations to live together. The females of the immediate and extended family did virtually all caregiving. If the housewife was ill, young unmarried relatives or spinsters moved in to help. This system was reinforced by religion and the frontier spirit. It took an extreme health problem to justify having a stranger care for the chronically ill. Only people without family, the 'furiously mad', or the very poor were not cared for at home. They were cared for in alms houses, jails, or shacks. Perhaps, this is the origin of loved ones not wanting to be placed and the guilt of families who find it necessary.

Men were not included in caregiving. They were bread winners and thought to be incapable of giving care. Today, the proportion of family caregivers who are male is increasing year after year. Still, it's seen as almost an oddity to imagine that a male could do the job.

Because the burden of caregiving was almost totally on women, their other contributions were curtailed. Just as today's caregiver loses income and becomes isolated, so did rural women caregivers in an earlier time.

The nursing profession evolved during the civil war. It grew to provide primary care for America by assisting families. Before 1920 nursing care focused on the entire person and his or her values. Nurses brought professionalism and service to the family and patient. The emphasis was often on palliative care, as most lingering disease ended in death. Saving the patient was a hoped-for result but rarely expected. This system of health care, except for the introduction of nursing, was close to the agrarian norm since the beginning of time.

Tuberculosis, plus an understanding of germs, infection, and technology changed everything. When tuberculosis was discovered to be contagious and caused by germs, it was found useful to remove the patient from home. This prevented infecting others and placed them in a clean environment to better recover. As a result, sanitariums and hospitals were built. They were cleaner and provided specially trained staff who provided care. The developing medical profession was now in charge and came to control the type of care and its delivery to patients.

This began the profound separation of family from health care. Strangers replaced the family. Many patients felt cut off from family. As time in a sanitarium crawled by, families didn't visit and write as often. Patients created new bonds with other patients and staff.

Technology and cost of equipment, along with detailed treatment protocols required centralization in hospitals. Nurses who earlier in the century assisted the family in the home, came to identify more with doctors in a hospital than families at home. They learned procedures to gain acceptance and respect. As a result, the nursing culture became more like physician culture. They gave less support to the family because their focus was on assisting the doctor to complete his procedures.

Health care policy accelerated this cultural change by paying for hospital procedures and not paying for interacting with family. Today, payment systems direct procedures for specific body parts and care is delivered in a programmed way. The patient and the family's role in decision making has been diminished along with caregiving. Doctors and nurses became pieceworkers focusing on the short-term, acute-care patient goals.

Family members are sometimes seen as in the way and discouraged from visiting. We still find some staff quick to judge visitors as difficult, if they stay too long and ask too many questions. Family presence reduces efficiency and takes time away from billable tasks. In today's new Intensive Care Unit there are so many machines and procedures that families are mostly restricted. Near death, doctors and nurses can't be maximally efficient if the family gathers around the bed. Doctors and nurses encourage visitors to go home and wait. "We'll call you if there is a change." Not only are families out of the way, it is easier for professionals to get away from one patient to attend to another. Families are less often present at death and lose the profound connection to death.

When a hospital stay is over, patients are discharged, often with inadequate instructions or follow-up. At discharge, the family is often short-changed. The convalescent plan is not aligned with family resources. It won't work if the patient needs continual care or caregivers live far away or need to be at work.

Cultural changes outside of health care have also had a profound effect on caregiving. Changes in family structure over the last 50 years have made home care more difficult. More women are in the workplace and delaying childbearing. Family size is smaller than it used to be. With later births, there are more often children at home when a parent might also need help. Higher divorce rates and dispersion of the nuclear family have reduced the ability and the willingness of family members to help.

People live longer now and diseases that appear later in life, such as Alzheimer's and Parkinson's, are much more common. We don't have the role models of past generations who provided care for the elderly. These cultural changes along with an increase in these diseases are overwhelming the health-care system. Family caregivers live in the here and now with emotional strain, social isolation, and exhaustion.

You are a friend, parent, spouse or child who cares for a loved one at the end of life. You make tremendous sacrifices without pay over years as your loved one declines and dies. It may be the most challenging and emotional thing you ever do. To be sure, the caregiver journey is difficult and harrowing. You wouldn't wish it on anyone. But you are committed to caring, because it is the right thing to do.

You will most likely outlive your loved one and personally grow from your experience. According to a 2017 survey of family caregivers, two-thirds of us find substantial benefits along the way. Half report a growth in confidence and feel more able to deal with difficult situations and make good decisions. Two-thirds become closer to their loved one, and 9 out of 10 are satisfied their loved one was well cared for. These statistics are encouraging.

We describe six phases of the caregiver journey, each with the emotions you may feel and the decisions you will face. Breaking the journey into phases helps you understand what is ahead and gives you a sense that there will be an end and you will be a good caregiver and survive the experience.

The stories will help you identify with - and learn from - people who get it. Each story is written by a caregiver who has lived and survived the experience. The exhaustion, isolation and depression that you feel are all here. The stories also describe how to cope: how some family members and friends provide real help and others don't. Few people understand what you are going through; some health-care professional are helpful, but a few are not. Well-meaning people ask about your loved one but seldom, ask how you are coping.

These caregiver stories begin with a suspicion of memory loss or other strange behavior that could indicate something is terribly wrong. Then, other changes appear, like mood changes, falling, or inability to perform familiar tasks. You learn to adjust and before long, you take over tasks your loved one used to do. The weight of your burden grows. It starts to take a toll. You are exhausted most of the time and don't sleep well. You realize caregiving is taking over your life and you may feel trapped. You learn you can't do it all by yourself and you reach out for help.

A time may come when you place your loved one in a nursing home or memory care unit. You struggle with staff and healthcare workers to get the best care possible. The end comes and you experience death and grief. You process what has happened and tentatively start to fill the void and reenter the world.

These phases and stories will help you better understand your journey. We hope you will feel less alone and better able to do the best you can. There is life after caregiving, and you will read how these caregivers succeeded. When it is over we hope you will be able to say you have no regrets and believe you did the best you could.

When a doctor or neurologist diagnoses a terminal disease, there are two people who need care, the patient and the family caregiver. Care professionals who read this book will be able to help caregivers take better care of themselves and their loved one. The health care system must consider the caregiver's health, capabilities, and limitations to provide necessary care in the home setting. After all, home caregivers put in more time and make more health decisions than anyone else.

This book is for family caregivers. It is written to you and for you. We have organized caregiver stories into the following phases and chapters:

1. Realize: My life will never be the same

Natural aging is one thing, but your loved one is not himself and you fear something is dreadfully wrong. You talk to a doctor. A diagnosis confirms a dreaded disease. You are shocked that your planned future may never happen, and your loved will leave you all too soon.

2. Commit: I can handle this

At first the burden is light, and you are determined to take care of your loved one. But you soon learn that the caregiver burden will dominate your future for many years.

3. Reach out: I need help

The burden will eventually wear you out physically, emotionally, and mentally. Caregivers find help with counselors, support groups, coaches, and in-home help to provide care. You also recognize that you must take better care of yourself.

4. Delegate: We need help

You will become so exhausted and worn out that both of you will need professional help. Home Health Care and Hospice Care enable you to continue taking care of your loved one at home for as long as you are able. You begin to let professionals lift the burden.

5. Advocate: I advise and protect

How do you know when it is time to place your loved one into a care facility? When the time comes, you will change jobs from being the caregiver to working with professionals. You become an advocate, their voice and protector who oversees others.

6. Grieve: I remember and adjust to a new life

You grieve each loss as you see your loved one slowly fade away. You have many wonderful memories and remember some horrible moments. Even though he or she is physically gone, your memories will remain. The memories are part of you and you will cherish them. Your grief will awaken your spirit to move on with your life, unencumbered with caregiving responsibilities. You are released to live again.

You made a commitment to care for your loved one. This is one of the highest callings of your lifetime. Taking care of yourself is not selfish. It is necessary to provide good care. You will succeed.

Chapter 1

Realize: My life will never be the same

Do you ever misplace your car keys or cell phone? Do you ever lose your train of thought? Do you forget someone's name a millisecond after you are introduced? If you have these senior moments join the club.

Aging is a normal process denied to many people, but it comes with new life experiences. Thanks to modern medicine we live longer than our grandparents. One of the downsides to living longer, however, is the appearance of frightening words like Alzheimer's, Parkinson's, stroke, dementia, and other diseases often associated with aging.

The early symptoms of these devastating diseases are difficult to distinguish from normal aging. It usually takes quite a while to suspect that something other than aging is causing an atypical behavior or memory loss. The realization that something is dreadfully wrong is devastating. Your mind races, you lose sleep and are overwhelmed with nightmares of caring for your loved one for the rest of your life. Retirement dreams are ruined and your financial nest egg, if you have one, may be eaten up by long-term care. You ask yourself, "What about me?" and then you feel guilty.

Therefore, you stumble around learning about the disease, notifying family, and crying every night. No wonder some caregivers find this first stage the most emotionally wrought of the entire journey. There is hope and a future, but you can't even imagine beyond a life of caregiving.

At some point you emerge from the initial brain fog and begin to adapt. Some tasks seem small and others large, like rocks in a backpack. Every new task adds another rock. It is not just the weight of the burden, but the fact that you will carry it for a long distance over some pretty rough terrain. It is going to wear you out.

You carry this burden wondering if all your remaining years will be dedicated to being a caregiver. You may stumble around in a daze, feel lost, and very alone. You don't know who to turn to, nobody seems to understand, and people who have never been in your shoes keep telling you what to do.

As you get to know the caregivers through their stories we hope you will understand yourself better. Picture yourself now in a support group, gleaning ideas that you can put into your caregiver toolbox. Some stories will continue in later chapters as each caregiving journey develops.

Realize: My life will never be the same

Ted-Our retirement plans went awry
Max-What's the matter with her?
Mary-I couldn't get him to take care of himself.
Rosa-Long distance caregiving was getting to me
Bonnie-I felt like I was in prison
Fred-I was in shock
Charlotte-The Parkinson's was taking him away
Roger--The humor and horror of it all
Joanne-I have Alzheimer's
Jerry-She's teaching me how to care for her
Faye-We were really isolated
Brenda-Life was unraveling
The Forest View

Our stories begin with a familiar scenario. When we are young we have dreams of the future. We plan our retirement and investments to allow us to travel or move to that place where we have always dreamed of living the remainder of our lives. The time arrives when those dreams and plans come to fruition and the day we retire dawns. Happy days turn into years and then your loved one begins to change. At first you begin to wonder: Are we just getting older and having senior moments, or is something seriously wrong?

Ted's story

Flo and I planned to move away from the big city to a rural area when we retired. We wanted to live close to nature and away from the hustle and bustle of the big city. The only problem was that we moved farther away from our children and stepchildren and their kids.

The years went by and we were living the life we had planned. We made new friends and enjoyed all our old activities as well as new hobbies. We started doing volunteer work, which we found most rewarding.

Then it began happening ever so gradually, barely noticeable at first. Flo was becoming more forgetful. She was misplacing things like her purse, car keys and cell phone. One day she got lost in our small town while she was driving to have coffee with her girlfriends. Then she could no longer remember how to prepare food; and she forgot to turn the stove off and could have burned the house down. She had always been a laid back, happy, and talkative woman but was now becoming withdrawn and at times sullen and negative.

Then one day as she was looking out the window, she told me she saw a man out on the sidewalk and was afraid. I assured her no one was out there and that started an argument. I knew that something was wrong, but I passed it off.

The forgetfulness and weird behaviors became more concerning and I couldn't deny that she was getting worse. Even Flo admitted that her memory was failing, and I keyed in on that by suggesting that we go to a doctor to see if there was anything he could do.

Our doctor gave Flo a very simple memory test and told her she had some memory issues and she should go to a neurologist to get a better idea of what was going on. The neurologist ordered an MRI (magnetic resonance imaging) and further tests. He diagnosed her as having a type of palsy. She had already had the disease for several years, but he said that the last few years would be the most difficult to live with. The neurologist explained that Flo's brain was losing some ability to remember recent information and events and that would affect her ability to reason and make decisions.

We left the office and I felt overwhelmed. What is happening? What do I do now? How long is this going to continue? The questions kept piling up, but I had no answers. The big question: What about me? Is the rest of my life going to be nothing but taking care of her? Even just the thought brought on a wave of guilt. I have loved and shared my life with this woman for 46 years and no matter what it takes, I will take care of her. *Ted's story continues in Chapter 2.*

Max's story

Normal aging has its rewards for a life well-lived and overcoming adversity with positive results. Older people have had experiences by which they evaluate the world around them. They know when things are normal and when they are not. This next story is typical of what most of us experience when faced with the dilemma: Is this aging or something more serious?

Bertie and I met 28 years ago when we worked in the same mortgage business and we got married soon afterwards. A few years ago, I began noticing her short-term memory loss and that her responses in social situations were slightly off. Her brother and sister who hadn't seen her for a year or more actually picked up on her deteriorating mental decline faster than I did. They asked me if I had noticed the change and I made up lame excuses for her behavior.

Then one day at work, when I asked her to look at a file with me, I paid more attention to her reaction. I realized that she had no idea how to read or understand what she was looking at. This was a huge change. I mustered up the courage to discuss this with her. I really did not want to tell her that her memory loss was a noticeable problem, but of course I thought I should tell her. It was a relief when she agreed there was an issue.

I suggested it might be helpful if we talked to someone who might be able to help us, so we made an appointment with a neurologist. I was nervous about that first meeting and how she would handle it.

He gave Bertie some memory tests and was extremely tactful and helpful. He diagnosed her with Mild Cognitive Impairment (MCI) and explained that this disease would most likely develop into dementia. He really didn't sufficiently explain what all those words meant, except that there was no reversing the progression of the disease. Her brain was dying.

He said that it might be worth trying some memory-enhancing drugs even though they don't work for everyone. He explained that the drugs may only briefly prolong the inevitable loss of memory and the side effects can make one miserable. But we decided to try two prescribed memory enhancement drugs for two years, until Bertie had some serious intestinal complications that put her in the hospital. I took her off those drugs and she immediately felt better. I don't think they did her any good at all. Her memory continued to decline, but it's anyone's guess if the medication slowed the progress or not.

I had to change employers, because I did not want to have to leave Bertie alone all day. I transferred to another employer nearer to home. Bertie stopped cooking and doing housework. It was a great relief when she voluntarily quit driving without anyone suggesting she do so. I could leave her home for half a day and feel comfortable that she was safe. I was gradually adapting to our changing lifestyle.

We have always been active in our church and enjoyed the fellowship. Just being with people of like faith is one of the highlights of our week. Then one Sunday morning I was all ready to leave and I checked in on her and she just sat in front of her mirror and said, "I'm not going to church anymore!" I dared not leave her alone, so we missed going to church.

Another Sunday she changed her mind and we got ready for church. She walked out of the bedroom and her bra was upside down and outside her blouse. I asked her if she would please put her bra on first and she got mad and said, "Why would I want to do that?" We didn't go to church that morning either.

More recently she started to interact with television programs. She sat there for hours watching and listening to programs and she talked to the actors as though they could hear her and respond. I stayed out of it and let her enjoy what pleased her. I figured I can get on with what I want to do if she is occupied.

Our conversations have changed. She has always been a positive person, but now it seems that no matter what we talk about her most-used word is "No." I feel sad and depressed that I am giving up my relationships with the other important people in my life to her disease. I'm a people person and my caregiving caused me to lose some of my social life, so I decided to do something about it - and found three other caregivers! We got together for coffee and shared what is going on at home. Word got out in our church and more have started coming. It is so encouraging to be with other caregivers going through the same things. We understand each other and after our meetings I feel uplifted.

I am coping well currently. I am looking down the road, however, knowing that she is going to get worse and I don't know how well I'll be able to take care of her. We don't have the finances to pay for long-term care, so I think I'll start looking into applying for Medicaid before she really needs it. I've also set up a meeting with an attorney to help guide me through the maze of Medicaid paperwork. I don't want to experience any complications if at all possible. I am frustrated and yet I feel good that I'm on the right track and I will get through this.

Mary's story

We do not grow up in perfect families and we certainly don't live in a perfect world. This is also the case with marriages, families, and all relationships. Caregivers rise out of all three groups, as do our loved ones. We get into the caregiver "business" with different motivations, but we commit, for whatever reason, to care for another person.

David and I worked hard at our marriage and it was a good one, if I did not rock the boat. We had 30 years of working together to make a success of our businesses. We always shared our working life and the raising of our sons. He was a controlling husband and father and kept our sons dependent on him in a successful attempt to control them, even into adulthood. I had the strength and boundaries to stand up to him.

David's health had been failing for a number of years. He had Type 2 diabetes and congestive heart failure. I first noticed his swelling ankles and told his doctor about it. He did have some dementia symptoms, and it was obvious that he had lost some short-term memory and cognitive ability. When I questioned his judgment, it was like stirring up a hornet's nest.

I was concerned about his health but not in a panic. He would not follow medical advice and that made me feel helpless, angry, and disappointed. I began to realize that being his caregiver was going to impact my freedom and future.

David was in total denial that his physical and mental illnesses even existed. That was frustrating and sometimes infuriating, because I couldn't reason with him. He never did admit that he had a memory problem. The boys and I never knew when he was forgetful or was covering up his memory loss.

I was upset because I couldn't get him to take better care of himself and as his illness worsened, I felt like a failure. As ten years passed it was harder and harder for me to be sympathetic and I became more impatient, which led to arguing all the time. I wasn't a happy camper. I didn't like what is happening to me and was fearful of the future. *Mary's story continues in Chapter 2.*

Rosa's story

How precious it is to see love manifested by caring for a loved one at the time of their greatest need. What an honor it is to return the love and devotion that was given to us. We cannot appreciate the sacrifices a parent makes to provide for us until later in life. On the other hand, it takes a different kind of love to care for someone you resent. Caregiving requires sacrifice and to give that to our loved ones without expectation of reward is the ultimate form of loving.

My father was a beloved outgoing community leader; a gentle, accomplished and jovial man. He gradually became reclusive and angry, which was a 180-degree turn from his lifelong personality. He started having episodes of forgetfulness and confusion. He got lost driving in the small community where he had lived for more than 30 years.

I was frustrated, because living in another state kept me from being there for him. Historically, my mother was domineering and unkind to my father. As he grew more confused, she goaded him into running errands that he could not complete to her satisfaction. She berated him in front of family and friends. She had always lifted herself up by putting him down. I felt sad that I could not be more present in their lives.

It helped to fly home once a month and talk to him about the changes I was seeing. He acknowledged that he was becoming like his own mother who had, in her old age, developed what was then called "senility". His mantra became, "When I get like that just shoot me." And: "Don't ever put me into a nursing home." *Rosa's story continues in Chapter 5.*

Bonnie's story

The goal of the early stages of caregiving for someone in the early stages of neurological diseases is to help them maintain the highest quality of life that they can enjoy. We try our best to make it easier on them, while unwittingly sacrificing ourselves. The love reservoir is being drained and there is no love refilling it. Relationships have their ups and downs, but when the trend is down and away, it takes a special devotion to carry the caregiver burden; however, there are limits to our endurance.

Ben and I worked in the same office as social workers for 25 years. He was an outdoorsman who enjoyed hunting, fishing, and just about any other outdoor activity. He tied his own flies and built handcrafted bamboo fishing rods. He was strict about gun safety. He was also concerned about the environment and was a follower of Aldo Leopold, the father of modern ecological principles for natural resource management.

I began to notice changes in his demeanor and behavior. He couldn't concentrate on any one thing for very long. He would sit and stare into space for long periods of time. It was becoming obvious to me that his short-term memory was declining.

Ben knew something was going on in his brain. I think he was more sensitive to early changes because of his experience as a social worker. He independently sought out memory testing and evaluation. I had noticed that he was not remembering things we had talked about, and occasionally forgot the meanings of words. He was initially diagnosed with Mild Cognitive Impairment.

The following year, many more issues began to crop up. He had difficulty remembering how to cook the simple dishes he had been making for years. When we went to a clinic for me to have eye surgeries, he couldn't remember how to get around the facility. He was unsure how to go from our hotel room to the surgery center by himself. He could not remember things we had done in our 15-year marriage or even with our professional colleagues.

Early on I was dismayed and had some regrets. We had a high-maintenance marriage and I regretted that I had not chosen to divorce long before his diagnosis. I felt trapped. As a social worker in a hospital setting, I had training and experience to work with people with dementia. I knew all too well what was in store for both of us.

I helped clients deal with their problems, but I had no emotional attachment. I didn't take their pain home with me. For me, caregiving at home soon became 24/7 and there was no relief from the stress. I was scared and worried about our capacity to physically, emotionally, and financially manage the care that would be needed.

We live out in the country away from town and family. There is no local care network and that worried me. I worried about isolation and I was so lonely. I worried about becoming impoverished in my old age due to the cost of his care. I was fearful because my husband had shown a capacity for violent language and wondered as his symptoms progressed whether he might lose his ability to control his feelings. I was feeling a lot of stress and anxiety and was coming to the point that I knew I was going to need some help. *Bonnie's story continues in Chapter 2.*

Fred's story

Fred was a goal-oriented person who searched for information upon which to base his decisions. He discovered that the amount of information available today on the Internet as well as from many foundations was not only overwhelming but can also lead to analysis paralysis. He found that it was important to understand what he was facing, but there came a time when he had enough information to make good decisions based on what he had learned. Fred would learn to adjust to his new role.

I met Bridget on a blind date. She had a radiant smile and won my heart. She told me, after we fell in love, that she had dated 87 young men and I was the best. She also liked that my last name started with "M", because hers started with a "W" and she was always next to last in line at school. She earned a bachelor's degree in business management.

Bridget worked to put me through graduate school, and we had a rather businesslike relationship, both working hard and saving for retirement. Being a mother was not easy for her; her low level of empathy that came from her upbringing made for a strained relationship, but we hung in there.

Bridget suffered from moderate to severe anxiety for which she had been taking medication since she was 30. After age 50 she began having insomnia and needed the television on all night. She got to where she refused to have her blood pressure taken before a surgery, because she feared our insurance might deny her claim. She thought only of herself; I suffered from a lack of intimacy, yet I remained faithful.

Before long she was changing before my eyes. She had always enjoyed getting out but now became unwilling to leave the house. She began hoarding things and seemed to be getting more and more anxious and more unreasonable. I didn't want to alarm her and make her more defensive and anxious by mentioning her behaviors.

I wrote a letter to her physician and asked her to evaluate Bridget and listed some behaviors such as saying "No" to any suggestion, not wanting to cook, and being unresponsive in bed. Bridget didn't want me to go with her to see the doctor, so I waited in the car. Her physician administered a memory test and referred her to a neurologist. When Bridget came out to the car, she was angry, "I answered all her questions and so I don't need a neurologist."

I suggested we go see the neurologist anyway, just in case. I was in the room for the neurological exam. I was embarrassed for her, because she couldn't answer most of the questions. I didn't like the way the doctor talked to me as if my wife was not in the room. A follow-up appointment gave us the bad news. The MRI revealed a shrinking ~~of one~~ lobe in her brain. He told Bridget, "You have the brain of an 85-year-old. You have dementia." For me that announcement was like hearing a judge say, "I sentence you to a life of caregiving with no possibility of parole." My life was already in shambles and I was devastated by the thought of life getting worse. Bridget was 66 and I was 67 at the time and that news did not sit well with either of us.

I was in a state of shock for a long time. When the numbness wore off, I felt our life together was over, particularly because she never would acknowledge that anything was wrong. You might call it denial, but in my search for understanding I came across the medical term, "anosognosia" (pronounced: a-no-sog-NO-sha). This Greek word is translated, "unaware of disease." The brain is unaware that anything is wrong. It is not denial, because people in denial know there is a problem but for many reasons avoid dealing with it. In either case, reasoning with her accomplished nothing but increase her anxiety. My problem was that we could not even talk about the most threatening thing that had ever happened to us. I had no one to talk to who could understand and I felt so alone.

Being an over-the-top intellectualizer, I googled everything and found lots of information, most of it not helpful. After several weeks I talked to a social worker at the Alzheimer's Association. I asked, "When can I shake some sense into her and say, 'We have to talk about this awful thing!'"

She gave me the hardest advice I could imagine, "Don't ever bring it up. It will only upset her. If she brings it up, you might softly discuss it." I was terribly frustrated by her response because I thought I could only help Bridget by discussing the situation. Now I could never discuss how to handle what I thought was the end of our relationship and our shared future. We never discussed it. Her life was better for it, but I was devastated. It took me a while to realize I couldn't fix her, but I was determined to take care of her to the very end. *Fred's story continues in Chapter 2.*

Charlotte's story

Charlotte's husband Carl was showing early symptoms of Parkinson's disease. She watched as he began having muscle tremors, rigidity, slowed movement, change in posture, weakened facial muscles, shuffling gait, and was delusions at times. Later he began having memory loss. Charlotte has never faced a greater challenge than caring for him. No matter the disease, it is the caregiver who commits and adjusts to this very difficult caregiving task.

Carl loved to hunt, fish, and garden. We pulled our trailer around the country and enjoyed life together. He was a voracious reader of history and the southwest. One day I noticed that he was just staring at his book. Parkinson's is not always apparent for often months or years before it is finally diagnosed. Carl had been having cognitive issues which were simply assumed to be because of his age, but we now know were Parkinson's related. The tremors, balance, and walking difficulties did not become a severe problem until later.

When I realized that he was not safe at home alone, I arranged for home healthcare services twice a week, which allowed me to get out of the house, play a little tennis and run errands. Our healthcare nurse was a godsend. I'm sure that I would have become depressed and angry about life if I were trapped at home caring for Carl without those few hours of freedom a week. I still worried about him when I was gone but reminded myself that he was being cared for. All this time I was withdrawing from my friends and life in general. I felt more and more alone. *Charlotte's story continues in Chapter 2.*

Roger's story

Experience is the best teacher and when it comes to caregiving we just don't have the experience to understand what is going on. Some do have the benefit of having been associated with others who have walked this caregiver road. Roger had been a long-distance caregiver for his mother and eventually placed her into a nursing home. A year after his mother died, he began to see familiar behaviors in his wife, short term memory loss, confusion, and becoming disoriented. Caring for a spouse is very different from caring for a parent. He was still not equipped to handle being a home caregiver for his wife.

Betty Jo and I met in a singles group. We had a lot in common and enjoyed each other's company. We married and after I retired we pulled our travel trailer across America. We enjoyed that lifestyle for about five years and then things began to change.

It was the middle of the night in 2001 soon after the 911 attack at the World Trade Center. President Bush had just announced that troops were being deployed to Afghanistan. I was sound asleep when she woke me up and said, "There's an airplane at the end of the block loading up soldiers to go to Afghanistan." I told her she was dreaming and go back to bed.

Betty Jo's short-term memory was deteriorating and she admitted it. At first I thought that forgetfulness and short-term memory loss was just because we were getting older. We went to a neurologist who tested her and ordered an MRI. He diagnosed her with 'Mild Cognitive Impairment' (MCI). He explained that her brain was losing its ability to store new information and therefore she couldn't recall it. She could remember details of long past events in great detail.

Her psychiatrist suggested we try a couple of the memory enhancing drugs that might help her short-term memory. She took them briefly until she had some uncomfortable side effects and there was no noticeable improvement. Her mental capacity continued to decline.

She had suffered anxiety depression much of her adult life and was under the care of a psychiatrist. Her medications did control her depression most of the time. The symptoms of dementia intensified. She began to hallucinate, was disoriented, and seemed her whole personality was changing into a shell of the person I knew. Before long we had to stop traveling and I blamed her for not being able to do what we had both enjoyed.

Just a couple weeks after the troops going to Afghanistan episode, she woke me up again and told me to get dressed, because we had to go to a baby shower. It was one o'clock in the morning and I asked, "Who's having a baby?"

She answered, "I am." Boy, howdy, I woke up!

I reasoned with her, "You said you had a hysterectomy 40 years ago and I had a vasectomy at least that long ago. If we pull this off, we have Abraham and Sarah's miracle (recorded in the Bible) beat."

"You're right. We'll have to adopt, because I don't want to let the people down who are having the baby shower."

I asked, "Do you really want to have a baby at our age?"

She replied, "Heavens no!"

I said, "Good, let's go back to bed." So I tucked her in and by the time I got back into bed, she was sound asleep. I didn't sleep the rest of the night. I wasn't worried about becoming a daddy but had a feeling that I was in for the long haul of being a caregiver and I was scared.

Between depression and dementia her behaviors were driving me nuts. I didn't know what to do. I felt trapped and it got to the point I couldn't leave her alone for even a few minutes. She followed me everywhere I went in the house. There was no escaping. I couldn't stand to live with her or without her and yet I was so desperate to escape that I even thought of divorce. I love her but what about me? Am I going to do nothing else but take care of her 24/7 for the rest of my life under these circumstances? *Roger's story continues in Chapter 2.*

Joanne's story

Caregivers cope with many aspects of diseases and resultant behaviors. We question why and rarely think about what is going on in the mind of a loved one. The following story is told by a person who has Alzheimer's disease. What is it like to live with this dreaded affliction? People react differently, but Joanne chose to bless her partner Jerry by realistically facing her inevitable journey by not burdening him with guilt or trying to control him. Rather, she told him how best to address her emotions and anticipated inappropriate behaviors.

I knew that my memory was getting bad so Jerry and I went to a neurologist. He ordered an MRI and gave me several tests. I really wasn't surprised when he told us that I was in the early stage of Alzheimer's disease. The results weren't unexpected and what I really wanted to hear, but it was still an emotional shock. We knew that we had to begin planning for what the future would lead to when full blown disease would be upon us. I have progressed on that road over the past three years and while I hate it, I also know that it is up to me how I continue to deal with it and at what point I have to give up making my own decisions about my future. Luckily Jerry is with me all the way. It has not been easy for him to have to watch and deal with my decline.

When I can't remember what he said 30 seconds ago, and he forgets and gets a little put out, I just say, "Jerry, look at who you are talking too," and we both try to laugh and just go on. I wish that every person with these problems could have such a loving and caring partner as I do.

As one who has Alzheimer's, let me tell you that it is scary at first, but I've kind of gotten used to it. Not that I like it, but once you have it you can either accept it and find ways to deal with it, or you can be angry all the time and make yourself and everyone around you miserable.

I live in a small town where I know almost everyone, some from the time they were children. I refuse to live in a social bubble. The problem is that I recognize faces, but I don't remember their names or how I know them and anything about them. That could make one crazy and not want to go out of the house.

When this first started I decided it was up to me to tell people I knew about my problem. I asked them that whenever we ran into each other to please tell me their name and sometimes how I knew them. And they do. I've told a few old friends to not ask me to guess their names, because that embarrasses me.

I do all I can to lead at least a somewhat normal social life. One simply must give up feeling sorry for one's self and realize it is up to you to decide how you want to attack the problems of "old age". When they say, "old age ain't for sissies" they are brighter than anyone knows until you get there.

Don't be afraid, just attack it head on and find your own way to deal with whatever old age brings to you. I would say, "Easy for me to say" but it isn't. It's a challenge every day to not become so depressed that you just want to check out. But I have found, at least for now, that no matter how difficult it continues to get, so far living is still worth it. Anybody who knows me knows that I am the furthest thing from a "Pollyanna" as one could get. I'm just saying, don't give up too soon.

There are still things I can do for myself, my friends, my community and others. Just hang in there for as long as you can stand it and then see what might happen. We are all going to go some time, just give everything you've got to give until then. It ain't going to be easy, but you can make the most of what you have left. I don't know how long I have before this dreaded disease will bring me to a vegetative state, and when that happens I probably won't care. I don't want to be put into an institution, but I guess I won't know one way or the other by that time, will I? So, there you are.

Jerry's story

Jerry has been Joanne's caregiver and walking the walk with her; starting when they hiked the mountain trails together, touring the country and enjoying retirement. Recently the trail has become steep and treacherous, but Jerry has been up to the task. He committed to being Joanne's caregiver:

Joanne has been the greatest blessing to me. She is one of the sharpest ladies I have ever known. When the Alzheimer's disease became apparent, she was braver than I could imagine. She has always been a very positive person and has an earthy and pragmatic approach to life.

When we got the diagnosis I was devastated. I didn't know what to say or do to comfort her. She comforted me! I was overwhelmed with sadness and so discouraged. Our future dreams and plans were gone. The big question in my minds was how fast the disease would take. How much time would we have to enjoy our relationship, before it is lost to the disease?

Over time Joanne realistically evaluated herself and suggested how I should cope with her for not only her benefit but also to relieve me of my guilt and anxiety. She has never backed off socializing and without embarrassment would tell someone that she had Alzheimer's and ask them to remind her of events that they had shared in the past.

Joanne used her writing skills to encourage others dealing with dementia-like diseases on Facebook. Because so many people knew her, they gave feedback to tell her that she was an inspiration. She didn't need that for her ego, but it was a blessing for her to learn that how her coping with the disease inspired them. We look forward to whatever quality of life remains and live it to the fullest.

The Forest View

The early stage of caring for a loved one begins to change your world. It is a huge adjustment to learn that a spouse, parent or any loved one has a terminal disease that will require years of care. The numbness and grief of a diagnosis is sometimes greater than the grief that comes from the loss of cognitive ability or even death. The complications of Parkinson's, stroke, Alzheimer's and other dementias are often overwhelming.

There are many new and uncharacteristic behaviors that might first alarm you. Some may seem like normal aging, especially remembering names or forgetting car keys. But there is a difference. It is one thing to forget the word for a can opener, but it is a big deal when one doesn't remember what a can opener does; your loved can't open a can of peas!

Uncharacteristic emotions and behaviors are a different matter. A normally mild mannered loved one who gets angry or uses swearwords for the first time is shocking. Some might start hording or refusing to visit close friends. You may react to the new behaviors in many ways. Some like Jerry reacted smoothly, because his wife accepted her diagnosis of Alzheimer's; he learned what was in the cards and worked in harmony to live with her disease. Others like Ted and Fred were devastated and overwhelmed by their unknown future and the loss of a planned life together. Some are dismayed that they can't, or don't want to do more, like Bonnie and Rosa.

Roger and Max's neurologist suggested drugs to improve memory. Their experiences are common that drugs probably won't help in the long run. Doctors are aware that the diagnosis is stark and want to soften the blow with something that might help. Caregivers are naturally eager to try anything that might help a love one's memory, even if it is only for a short time. The truth is that there are currently no approved drugs that stop or even slow down dementia. The drugs that are approved have side effects.

Some caregivers are so committed to fixing the disease that they spend lots of time and money on things that don't work. It takes time to learn that your goal is to comfort your loved one without you dying in the process. Some of these diseases such as Parkinson's do have effective medicines and medical procedures that may help in the short term. Regardless, the decision to try any drug is between you, your doctor, and your loved one.

Another component of our adapting is the degree of awareness your loved one has about the disease. Some patients like Joanne who has Alzheimer's, are very aware and want to help. Others like Bridget, Rosa's dad and David are either in denial or their brains just don't recognize that anything is wrong. The loved one's lack of awareness of the disease isolates caregivers when they most need support. It makes everything harder. On the other hand, loved ones who are aware often feel overwhelmed. They may be angry that their quality of life has been taken away. Their anger may be directed at you because you are close at hand.

After you get a diagnosis of a disease, there is much emotional upheaval, but you will begin to rearrange your life and relationships as you adapt. The disease will change your loved one and that will change you in ways you cannot imagine.

In the beginning, you aren't even sure what kind of help you need. You don't know what you don't know and therefore don't even know what questions to ask. You are so consumed by the here and now that it's hard to adjust to what is going on. Inevitably, a caring person will say, "Let me know how I can help" and it leaves you nonplused. "Take care of yourself" is often unappreciated by caregivers. The old adage: "How do you concentrate on draining the swamp when you are up to your hip pockets in alligators" is true for caregivers. You will wrestle a lot of 'gators and become quite adept at dealing with them, be it your loved one's behavior or people who simply don't understand.

What is Dementia, Anyway?

Dementia comes from the Latin "demens" for "out from one's mind". The word has been in general circulation for more than 100 years, and yet caregivers who are at the beginning of their journey struggle to know what it means and how it differs from Alzheimer's.

Many older Americans never heard about dementia when they were young. Because the occurrence of most dementias is related to age, the increasing population of people over 65 has dramatically increased the incidence of this malady. Since we don't know what causes most neurological brain diseases that result in dementia, it is hard to describe them.

Here's a simple way to look at it. The brain is an organ, like the lungs, liver, bladder, kidneys, heart, stomach, and intestines. A diagnosis of dementia means the brain is in organ-failure. Because organs are critical to sustaining life, dementia most likely will lead to death. Dementia is clinically diagnosed by noticing significant mental changes that interfere with daily activities. Doctors will look for mental deficits including memory loss, speech problems, reasoning errors and perceptual mistakes - all brain stuff. Usually after years of these worsening declines, the brain's limbic system, that controls appetite, the ability to walk, swallow, digest, and breathe, begin to fail. Although often called a disease, dementia is just a long list of symptoms.

Mild Cognitive Impairment (MCI) means there are some mental changes occurring, but the changes don't currently interfere with daily activities. Research is ongoing to determine the link between MCI and dementia, because it is not clear if MCI leads to dementia.

What causes dementia? This is where things get murky. Indeed, the medical community, including researchers and clinicians, know very little about the causes. Therefore, they have little to tell caregivers about what to expect and little to offer about coping with the behaviors.

Diseases such as Alzheimer's, stroke, depression, alcoholism and drug abuse, to name a few, are major causes of dementia. Alzheimer's is the cause for 60- 80% of cases, so it dominates research and public interest. The medical community has helped us understand more about the stages of Alzheimer's. It progresses from short-term memory loss to problem solving errors, to uncharacteristic emotions, to long-term memory loss, to incontinence, and other organ failures.

Upon diagnosis you want to know, "How long does my loved one have to live?" For Alzheimer's, the answer is from four to 20 years. Because each patient is unique, we don't know how the disease will progress. The older a person is when onset is diagnosed, the shorter the estimated life span. Other life-shortening factors are being discovered. Men have a higher mortality rate than women. Additional diseases piled on top of the disease, called comorbidity, shorten life expectancy.

Chapter 2

Commit: I Can Handle This

'Caregiver burden' is pretty light to begin with. Before long however, you assume more of the tasks your loved used to do, things like handling finances, taxes, driving, house or yard work. You know how to do many of the tasks because you shared them. The ones you haven't shared are more challenging. All these tasks add rocks to your backpack and it gets heavier. You notice the weight the longer you carry the load. You think about the hard jobs more than the easy ones. So you cut back on other things to save time and energy. You first delete things you used to do alone: hobbies, exercise, visiting friends, and perhaps reading. You prioritize your time and energy to accomplish the increased responsibility and before you know it, every fiber in your body is committed to caring for your loved one. You have very little time for yourself.

We have only begun describing the caregiver journey, and we can already identify one theme: your steadfast commitment to care for your loved one. We may be motivated by promises, religious vows, giving back to a heroic parent, the hunger to repay a loving spouse, or a strong desire to do the right thing.

Even with the tremendous challenges of committing to be a caregiver, it has tremendous rewards. You will have short-term and long-term rewards. You will feel good about yourself deep in your heart, even on those bad days. Strong commitment is required to sustain yourself on this journey and it will be tested by each and every demand. Caregiving teaches there will be an end to every life and it makes you appreciate every day more. You will learn that you have much less control of your life than you used to think you had. You gain self-confidence that you are rising to meet one of life's great challenges and provide the best care you can. You will create memories of small and large moments. You will draw closer to your family and friends in meaningful ways. We know that when your last days come, you will be more at peace than if you had not had this experience. Lastly, you will accept that you can't save your loved one and that you did the best you could.

The early phase of caregiving is hectic enough, but as your loved one's condition deteriorates, new problems arise that require innovative approaches to deal with the physical issues and the inappropriate behaviors. Your loved one's disease takes over both of your lives. Each disease has a different rate of functional decline because each brain and each person is different.

The emotional impact on you is like being on a rollercoaster. While the loved one's journey is downward, the daily grind of caring has emotional ups and downs. A wonderful day that is so close to normal it makes you wonder if the diagnosis was wrong. An hour later, a mood swing blows up in your face. You are anguished as your love, your dreams, and your hopes for the future fade. You are disappointed, angry, hurt and feel rejected.

This ride has many unexpected turns, dark tunnels of despair, and disorienting loop-de-loops in the forms of unexpected financial challenges, family disputes, failing health, and compassion fatigue. People you thought would support you don't. Your health takes a hit; on and on. It is impossible to be proactive. This ride ain't fun no more and you want to get off the rollercoaster.

Commit: I can handle this

Ted's story continues

Ted's wife had symptoms of early stage dementia. He was glad they got a diagnosis so he had some idea of what Flo was dealing with. That diagnosis shocked him to the core. He had a name for her disease but was already having trouble taking care of her and was so saddened to see her mind and body slip away, and there was nothing he could do to fix her. His life was changing and he didn't know what to do.

Flo had a form of palsy that began causing her problems walking. I walked along side of her and bought her a cane, but after another fall it became apparent that she was going to have to use a wheelchair. As she lost mobility, my workload increased dramatically. I gave up my golf, fishing, and didn't even have time to go out and have coffee with my buddies. She didn't want to go out and she resented my leaving her alone to go to the store. I took her with me most of the time to get her out of the house.

She got awfully bossy and I got sick and tired of her treating me like I was her slave. Sometimes I lashed out at her and told her to quit nagging me and then she would start crying. Then, I began hating myself for hurting the one I loved.

As her disease progressed I had to help her get dressed. She didn't want to shower and I was concerned about hygiene. She had always been a neat and tidy lady and then she got to the point she didn't care how she looked or what she wore. In one way it made it easier for me, because I bought her some nice sets of sweatpants and tops. She seemed happy with them and made it a whole lot easier for me to dress her.

We didn't go out in public, because she didn't want people to see her failed condition. I withdrew socially as well. I hated what was happening to me. I like being around people, but those who knew us withdrew from us. I felt so alone. I didn't have a wife whom I could converse with, because the disease soon took her ability to talk. People would ask, "How is Flo?" and never asked how I was doing. I was in worse emotional condition than my wife and it seemed like no one cared about me.

I was getting so tired and worn out. I'm a strong man and I thought I could handle it. After all, I knew her better than anyone else and it was up to me to take care of her. I don't know if it was my ego and pride, but I thought asking for help was a sign of weakness. But, like a bad toothache, I couldn't take it much longer. I did need help, but I didn't know how to go about it and I didn't even know what I really needed. *Ted's story continues in Chapter 3.*

Dwight's story

Dwight's siblings lived close to their mom and checked on her periodically, but they were busy with their lives and as her need for more help increased, they stepped back even more. Dwight had always been close to his mother and the caregiving responsibility fell upon him by default. He willingly made the commitment to be her caregiver. Having missed taking care of her in the early stage of dementia, we pick up his story as he began his caregiving journey.

I lived across the state from mom. My brother and sister had been observing that she was showing some symptoms of Alzheimer's. I had been driving over to see mom every two weeks to pay her bills and to take her shopping, because she is blind and could not do that for herself. She had learned how to live with her blindness and it was amazing how much she could do for herself.

I had little reason to stay where I lived and she needed someone around as much for companionship and to take care of the house. It worked out great for me to move in with her. I did not feel imposed upon and was never resentful or angry about taking care of her. Mom and I are cut from the same cloth, so we get along well.

I am single so I didn't have anyone close to me to talk to about my feelings and so I kept them to myself. Most of the family thought it was good for me to take care of mom, but it has always been a joy, not a job, to take care of her. It never entered my mind that taking care of her was what any person should do for a loved one.

The load began to increase when I went from doing general things around the house to more and more personal matters like helping her to the toilet and through the whole process. At first it felt very awkward, then just a little bit awkward. I was never actually comfortable parenting my mom.

Before long I gave up a lot of my personal life, but all in all I have been able to spend more time with mom and I don't feel that I had lost anything. There are so many things that a person doesn't know when they start down this path. I was afraid of the unknown like I was walking without a clue as to what I would face and being blindsided by unforeseen problems.

After I moved in with mom, I found a job and worked a regular schedule. I left meals in the refrigerator and snacks for her while I was gone. I could leave for a few days to go deer hunting or fishing and she could take care of herself while I was gone. This lasted for about five years and then she started to need more and more of my time.

She was starting to get more confused and even more forgetful about things. There came a point that I did not feel comfortable about leaving her by herself at night. I was afraid that she might fall or have some other accident. I slept with 'one ear open' at night listening for her moving around and always worried that she might fall. I gave up going out for an evening or overnight. I was becoming more housebound and I didn't like it,

My life started to change. I quit hunting and fishing and other things I had always enjoyed. I would have to find a family member to stay with mom if I needed to be away.

When I explained that I needed a break. My family really didn't understand what was really going on or why I needed them every now and then. Some of them seemed 'put out' to sit with mom although she was never a problem. I'll not judge them, because they each have their own issues about taking care of mom. I can't expect them to act the way I think they should.

At about year seven mom started having anxiety attacks. At first she would just be afraid of something that she could not describe. She would cry, scream, and yell for help. She wanted me right next to her so I could comfort her. This would happen once in a while and after 10 to 20 minutes she would be fine. Within a few weeks it was happening daily at all hours of the day and night. I was becoming her worn out security blanket.

Mom's dementia got to the point that she would wake up from a nap and forget that she was blind. She would scream, "Help me. I'm blind. I can't see. What's happening to me?" I would rush to her side and remind her that she had been blind for several years and then she would remember and calm down. I can only imagine having a vivid dream and waking up and not thinking I was blind. It would scare me to death. I felt so sorry for mom. The need for me to care for her got to the point that I left my job to take care of her 24/7.

Her symptoms escalated quickly. Her anxiety attacks started to happen more frequently and last longer (as much as 30 hours straight). I took her to the doctor to get medication that might help. One night she was having a particularly bad attack and the as needed medication was not working. By the next morning she was so caught in the grip of that attack and she couldn't get out of bed or even move. The thought of placing mom into a care center haunted me as my worst nightmare. I'd heard so many horror stories about nursing homes and I just couldn't bear to put her into a hell hole to die. But, in the back of my mind I knew that it wasn't IF she would get worse and I was losing her. My emotions were raw as my life was soon to take another turn. *Dwight's story continues in Chapter 3.*

Fred's story continues

Fred was becoming desperate and searching for ways to cope with his wife's behaviors. Knowledge alone was not helping him cope. The burden of caring for her had been bearable, but the increasing stress was beginning to change him and he didn't like what was happening.

We lived in Phoenix when Bridget was diagnosed. We returned to our summer home in Western Colorado a month later, so I had some time to think how to tell family and friends. I thought that was better than keeping her dementia a secret, partly because some folks had observed changes. It felt like it was the right thing to do. Everyone was kind and offered support. I was surprised that the friends I expected to be most supportive were not and casual friends sometimes went out of their way to take Bridget to lunch or bring a meal. Friends who have experienced dementia in their family were especially kind.

I got lots of mixed messages. At a potluck supper a friend expressed pleasure that I was out and being with others. But when she asked, "Where's Bridget?" things went sour.

I answered, "She's at home and safe there by herself."

Her face changed to a frown of displeasure, "Oh, that's not right. You wouldn't leave a child home alone, would you?"

Several tried to encourage me by saying, "Take care of yourself"' as they back away. I just bristle when I hear those empty words. I'd love to take better care of myself, if I could just get a complete night's sleep that would be a start.

The revelation of Bridget's changing came one Christmas season a few years ago. Bridget and I were decorating our three-foot, artificial tree. It's also a pathetic excuse for a Christmas tree. I found a working string of lights, a challenge, and asked Bridget to arrange them on the tree. I worked on something else for a while and returned to check on her progress. She had made none. In fact, she was holding the end of the string in exactly the same way, staring at the tree. She had forgotten how to string lights.

Then I said something I regretted later. I raised my voice. "What's wrong? Can't you do it? Never mind, I'll do it myself!" She seemed relieved. She did not notice the frustration in my voice, but I did.

Each evening just before bed, I meditate. That night I thought about the lights and why I raised my voice. I knew the outburst wasn't necessary or useful. It diminished Bridget and showed my anger and lack of control. It really sunk in that dementia was at work, stealing her ability to arrange things. Other losses were adding up, like getting lost driving to her mother's house.

I knew Bridget would get worse and that upset me every time some new behavior occurred, but I had problems accepting it. It popped into my head that I had made an emotional deal with Bridget: I will take care of you if you will not get worse. Seeing her staring at the lights after 15 minutes was evidence that she was not doing her part. I knew this was ridiculous, because nothing would have prevented her decline. I was lying to myself.

I was worried about her driving. She drove very slowly and would not take any suggestions. Luckily, Bridget didn't want to drive in new places or on freeways. She saw no reason she couldn't drive to her mother's home about three miles away. I hoped she would have a small accident, like backing into another car in a parking lot. That might frighten her and make her give up driving. She did scrape the front bumper backing out of the garage but pretended it didn't happen. One day she got lost driving to her mother's house, a trip she had made successfully for several years. She came home on her own. She was shaken and never asked to drive again.

It wasn't hard to take over the driving and do most shopping on my own if I had a good list. I liked fixing things in the house and the yard. It was useful to get a break away from the drama but at the same time, I felt so lonely. Those tasks became more like chores than building our future together. I was wearing out and decided to prioritize my energy by planting fewer annual flowers. Cutting back on housekeeping was easily accomplished. Our house soon showed my neglect and after a while I'd have to pay more attention to chores that I dreaded. This only added to my frustration.

Bridget had always done an excellent job of managing the bank account and paying bills. She handled all our finances and filed our income taxes every year. When she couldn't do it anymore, it fell upon me. I avoided doing our taxes to the point of filing an extension at the last minute. I got in the habit of procrastinating and then I'd feel bad about myself.

Even though I successfully cut back on the workload that in and of itself was emotionally depressing. As each season passed I could see how much more Bridget had slipped and emphasized my helplessness. As her caregiver I felt more and more ineffective. I played golf less. I watched whatever she wanted on TV. It was mind numbing. I noticed the house was wasting away as well as the two of us. I felt much older. Even though I have always been a positive person, a sadness came over me. I didn't like the way I was changing and I determined to overcome. *Fred's story continues in Chapter 3*

June's story

June's sister had been taking care of their mother for several years. Even though she kept June informed about their mother's worsening dementia, she couldn't believe it-not their mother. June couldn't understand the depth of her sister's despair. Although far away in miles, they were very close. June went back to give her sister a break. She was looking forward to enjoying the good times she had shared with her mom just a couple years before.

I grew up in a wonderful home and cherish the memories of mom, dad, and my sister. When I finished high school I moved out west to seek adventure and a life away from the big city. I married a wonderful man, raised our children and time seemed to pass so swiftly and before long we began to enjoy retirement.

My sister left home, married, and raised her family but always lived close to our folks. Dad died and left mom alone. As a widow she grieved the loss of dad, but she reached out and was active in her church and volunteered in the local hospital.

As the years went by I visited mom about once a year. My sister told me that mom was failing and that she needed more help to clean her house, do yard work, and drive her to appointments and shopping. When I went for a visit, I gave Sis a break and it was a joy to be with mom and run around together. I even enjoyed doing the chores with her. She was doing great in her old age.

I told Sis that she was doing a good job taking care of mom. When I got home I soon got busy with my life and before I knew it a couple years had gone by since I had seen mom. I was faithful to call Sis and ask how mom was doing. Sis told me that mom was diagnosed with dementia and was losing her short-term memory and was easily confused and disoriented. I couldn't picture mom failing like that.

Sis said that all she was doing was taking care of mom and that her husband was feeling neglected and she needed a break. I was excited to go back and be with mom and give Sis a break. I would be alone for two weeks with mom and was thinking about the fun things we had always enjoyed doing together and could do them again.
June's story continues in Chapter 3.

Bonnie's story continues

Bonnie's husband enjoyed the outdoor life. At times Ben functioned normally and then he began exhibiting more behaviors associated with Alzheimer's such as memory loss. Their marriage had been a rocky one and more of a convenient relationship. Yet, they remained together as Bonnie's story continues.

Ben's symptoms progressed and with his diagnosis of Alzheimer's about two years after his first assessment, I resigned myself to be his caregiver. Some of Ben's behaviors didn't fit the usual Alzheimer's diagnosis, so he agreed to have more tests. He is now diagnosed with "Frontotemporal Dementia", not Alzheimer's. There was confusion among the neurology doctors about his diagnosis because he didn't fit neatly into either Alzheimer's or major depression induced dementia, so he was referred to a new psychiatrist/neurologist.

He went over all the precursory signs, cognitive testing, MRI, CT, and PET scans showed how the diagnosis of Frontotemporal Dementia (FTD) fits. It matched with what I had been observing. And learned that FTD is often misdiagnosed for several years as either Alzheimer's or a psychiatric disorder. I'm SO relieved to have an accurate diagnosis and better road map for the future, although the latter is in some ways even more difficult to manage than Alzheimer's.

I began working on my emotional approach to caregiving, especially considering the past conflicts in our marriage, I couldn't do it with the kind of love that comes from a long and blessed marriage. Friends and family often questioned me in this stage about why I was choosing to stay with my husband to care for him. They knew he was easily angered, depressed and at times verbally abusive and he made some physical threats. I sought the advice and counsel of an attorney friend who pressed me to file for divorce while Ben was still considered mentally competent. I found it cathartic to write a short essay to myself, trying to figure out why I was choosing caregiving.

> There is a selfishness, a motivation for myself that leads me to enter this period of caring for Ben. I'm

> doing this for me at least as much as I'm doing it for him. Yes, I acknowledge that if I abandoned Ben, he and others with him would find ways to help him to get care when he needs it. His quality of life might be different, might be worse, and might be better. And I acknowledge that I could live with more imagination and broader practical opportunity without the responsibility of providing his care. But I would lose an opportunity for my own growth. I wouldn't learn something I need to learn. I don't think I see myself as his savior, as my counselor alleged. I believe I made a choice to join our lives, for many reasons. Having made that choice, I'm accepting that a choice was made by **me** and further choosing to find what it is I'm to learn through this. I'm accepting the challenge I've brought into my life by marrying Ben: it's there and it's OK. I accept that it will not be easy, simple or pleasurable. I'm challenging myself to learn how to create and sustain intention for presence, a sense of peace and loving kindness toward myself and another. If I were to run away from this opportunity to learn now, it will remain something I still need to face and learn. I want to learn and grow in spirit.

My role in this earliest stage was mostly to direct our future planning while Ben could participate in the decisions and process. Considering his diagnosis we had an attorney update our wills to protect our assets much as was possible. I made sure he completed and signed his Durable and Medical Power of Attorney authority over to me. I began having consistent and independent communication with his family and of course to keep my own family informed.

I tried to educate Ben about dementia as much as was possible. He didn't have a clue about its progression. He read one book about Alzheimer's. It was important to me that he understood the extent of caregiving that would be required in the future. I wanted him to participate in planning before he would be declared incompetent. I repeatedly explained the legal decisions over and over. He could understand now, but he couldn't hold onto that knowledge.

Ben was very independent and enjoyed outdoor activities like hunting and fishing that he had always enjoyed. After he retired he continued to hunt and fish and when home he enjoyed his collection of antique bamboo fishing rods, tied his own flies, and took meticulous care of his guns.

One day we went for a drive into the countryside. I noticed how his reactions were slowing and he scared me a couple times. I asked his Occupational Therapist to assess his driving skills. My insistence that he be tested paid off. It was not safe for him to drive in congested or fast paced traffic such as interstates or larger cities anymore. He could drive within short distances of home and to his favorite nearby fishing spots. I was so thankful that he abided by the limitations placed upon him.

He loved to go fishing and on one trip he didn't make it home until six o'clock the next morning. I spent a sleepless night in panic. Up to that point I was fearful every time he left the house, but I tolerated his going fishing and hunting, because he enjoyed the outdoors so much. Rather than lay down the law and setting boundaries for him, I adapted my response in a positive way.

I bought a Global Positioning System (GPS) so I could track his whereabouts no matter where he went. He continued to go to his favorite places, and I had some peace of mind knowing I could send people to rescue him if he got lost or hurt. Having guns in the house didn't bother me, because he kept them locked up and I knew where he kept the key. He has never hallucinated about seeing people or anything else that would alert me that he was becoming a danger to himself or others. His guns and fishing gear are part of who he is and I didn't want to take those away from him until it wasn't safe for him to have access to firearms.

My feelings about my caregiving role at this early point are gratitude that my job as a social worker helped prepare me for my husband's care and gain his cooperation in the process. I am also grateful for his independence and the freedom it gives me. Fear of losing my future was always present. I was grieving what I felt would be the loss of my old age that I'd hoped would include travel, learning, adventure, and companionship. I feel more prepared now for what is in my future.

Living in a rural area far away from resources that are more readily available in larger cities is something you learn to live with. Caregiving, however, becomes even more difficult. I did contact our AAA about some home care assistance. I don't need them yet, but it's good to know that some help is available when the time comes. We are more interdependent with our neighbors. It is part of our culture to look after each other and that is the quality of life that we have enjoyed here.

I can still take care of Ben at home, but I know the time is coming that I will have to place him into a care facility. I dread that time and yet I know it will be a relief for me as his caregiver. I feel a little guilty even thinking about placing him.

Linda's story

Linda stepped into the role of a caregiver for her mother without any knowledge of what was happening. By this time symptoms of dementia were becoming undeniable. Linda took on the all the responsibility for care and at first she was just frustrated but able to cope.

Mom's memory started to get bad. She started doing odd things like folding dirty clothes and putting them in a drawer or purchase a large quantity of things such as toilet paper or Q tips. She would go to the bank several times a week to find out her balances. I tried to explain to her that she wasn't remembering things correctly, she wouldn't accept that and get angry.

It wasn't immediately obvious that mom had dementia at first. It happened a little over time.

I just dug in and did what needed to be done at that moment or day to day. I was recently widowed, so when I asked mom to move in with me, as a companion. I didn't think about any future hopes or dreams at the time

At first, I took mom to our family doctor. He performed an in-office assessment which indicated she may have diminished mental abilities. He referred us to a neurologist that also did an in-office test, he diagnosed her with dementia with symptoms of Alzheimer's. He prescribed a medication which might help her memory but made her very ill. We decided not to use medication.

My family didn't help in any way. It was obvious they didn't want to be involved. The only help I got was from a friend who worked for the Area Agency on Aging. I attended a Caregivers Summit each year. That was the best help I received. I also got help with counseling and help at home when I needed a break. The family didn't visit often. I had a 90th birthday party for mom and they came for that. Mom was showing more signs of decline but no one would talk about it.

I was able to get someone scheduled to stay with mom when I wanted a break, but it was only a day here and there. As for the sleeping, it was like having a baby, I slept with one eye open. I even purchased a baby monitor so I could hear when she got up and used the bathroom.

I kept the family updated about her medical status. The family didn't really understand what that meant for me and her caregiver and didn't contribute in any way for her care, or my well-being. Mom was living in a senior apartment near my brother. She was always complaining how unhappy she was and that my brother wasn't helping her with anything. I had lost my husband and asked mom if she wanted to live with me since I was alone too. I moved her from the Front Range to my home on the west slope. *Linda's story continues in Chapter 3.*

Charlotte's story continues

Charlotte's caregiving journey started ever so slowly. Carl had Parkinson's for a long time before obvious symptoms began showing up that impacted on her. He was able to do most things for himself, but as the disease progressed he became more dependent and eventually totally dependent on her: Her 'caregiver burden' was getting heavier and dragging her down. She was alone and needed help.

Carl's physical and mental condition deteriorated further. He had always been a good communicator, but he quit making eye contact when he spoke, which was unlike him. It seemed like all at once he began choking on food, having poor posture, difficulty with balance and walking. I was concerned, but I didn't know those were symptoms of Parkinson's disease until I spoke with a family member who is a doctor. As Carl's difficulties increased, so did my anxiety level. There were times when I'd look at him and was totally terrified by what was happening to him. The lack of my ability to help him made me feel like a failure.

I thought it was important to talk to him about my observations but that was totally fruitless, because he was in denial and very defensive. If I did bring the subject up, he got very angry. I think he was scared and he lashed out at me. It was a big mistake thinking I could make him understand what was happening to him. He couldn't process any information I gave to him. I had to remind myself that it was the disease talking and not my man. When I separated the disease from the shell of the man I had known for so many years, my anxiety was lessened.

I was becoming more concerned about his increasing mental confusion and balance; problems that come with Parkinson's. I was scared not only for his safety, but increasingly was becoming frightened for my own safety, because when he felt he was not in control, he could become physically abusive to me.

I felt so alone and I didn't have anyone to talk to who understood what I was going through. I had no family in the area, but they were supportive over the phone. My stepdaughters visited as often as possible to provide some help. The physical and emotional load had become so great that I couldn't take it anymore. I decided to find some help. *Charlotte's story continues in Chapter 3.*

Mary's story continues

David had diabetes and congestive heart failure along with dementia. He could not admit that he had any memory problems. He would not cooperate with his doctors or Mary. His antagonism made it most difficult for her to care for him. She was committed to taking care of him despite his self-destructive nature. She was getting desperate as her story continues:

David never said it, but I believe he really wanted to die. I think he was becoming more apathetic, because he felt he had no purpose for living. He was very insecure and hated the thought of being dependent on me. He was always coming up with some way to restrict my activities and to stay at home to take care of him. His controlling nature intensified as did his dementia. At times I felt like I was incarcerated in my own home. I felt totally isolated and alone. I was resentful and would get so angry with him over some minor incident, because I had been storing up my pain. I was miserable.

Our family physician was helpful and I had some home care nurses come in three days a week. They were of tremendous help beyond their paychecks. They were frustrated by his unwillingness to cooperate. I had no other people who I could talk to and understood. The only support I had was from our sons who were empathetic towards me but angry with their father. They really didn't give me the support I needed and I didn't expect much from them. They had their own issues.

David thought he could still run our family business. I wish I would have stood up to him in that regard but at the time didn't seem worth the battle. His dementia was causing him to make unwise financial decisions and caused us to lose a lot of money.

His brothers and sister were not aware of his condition, because he could put on a convincing act whether they visited in person or talked over the phone. I finally brought them into the information loop so they knew the truth about his condition. Because we lived such great distances apart, they couldn't be of any practical help. Although they cared, I really felt no support from them. I did the caregiving my way and came out of it a better person.

I was never to the point where I thought of placing him into a nursing home and none would probably have accepted him, because he could turn violent. I took care of at home until one night he died quietly in his sleep. My caregiver journey ended and I looked forward to moving on with my new life. *Mary's story continues in Chapter 6.*

Roger's story continues

Roger's story started many years ago being a long-distance caregiver for his mother. About the time of his mother's death his wife began having some very familiar mental health issues. She admitted to having memory problems and together they sought help and he knew he was in for another long roller coaster ride.

Betty Jo began having wild hallucinations. She was obsessed with clothes. She grew up poor and even though she had two closets full of clothes (some even with the tags attached) she wanted more. She thought we had another house and her clothes were in in that house. The hallucinations are too many to mention, but they got so bad that I called her neurologist and told him things were getting out of hand and I couldn't handle it much longer.

He had me take her to a psychiatric hospital. The psychiatrist determined that one of her anti depression medications had become toxic and he also diagnosed her with Mild Cognitive Impairment (MCI) which was affecting her memory and contributed to her deteriorating mental condition, but he never mentioned the word "dementia." He gave me no clue as to what I was in for. I didn't even get a "Good Luck" when he released her.

I took her to a different psychiatrist who changed her medications and she calmed down. I took her home and she agreed to go to counseling with me. The next three months went quite smoothly and we got along fine. Before long however, she slipped back into her demented state and I was back on the roller coaster again.

I was working a part time job and one day she called my cell phone and said," I am in a run-down motel in Ruidoso, New Mexico, with four boys. You need to come get me." I knew she was calling from the house, so I left work. When I walked into the living room I was greeted by a very angry woman yelling at me, "Why did you leave me in this motel with four boys and no money?"

By this time I was getting used to her hallucinating and it didn't upset me. I asked where the boys were. She walked through the house and said that they must have left. About then she realized that she was home. I embraced her and didn't say anything. I let the matter drop. I quit my job so that I could be with her full time. *Roger's story continues in Chapter 3.*

Connie's story

'Tag-team' caregiving is one alternative to looking after a loved one by taking turns and sharing responsibility. This works when the team members are on the same page, working for the same goals, respecting and trusting each other and sensitive to each other's strengths, weaknesses, and limitations. When it comes to adult children caring for a parent they may not understand that within our hearts are feelings toward a parent or sibling that have never been known to anyone else. There may be feelings of very deep love or hidden resentment. These may surface in how we react when it comes to caregiving decisions.

Connie's mother was living at home and taking pretty good care of herself, but as she aged she needed help with more chores around the house. She was letting a lot of issues slide as her cognitive ability began to wane. Connie and her brother had to start picking up the slack.

Mom had lived happily and independently in her own home since dad died over 10 years ago. She lived alone and handled all her affairs, kept a clean house, loved working in her garden and yard, and prepared enough meals for herself. My brother and I were the only family she had and we lived close enough to visit frequently. Her grandchildren lived out of the area but phoned her regularly and visited when they could.

We began noticing a mental decline when she couldn't seem to follow a familiar recipe or keep track of characters in a book. Out of frustration she gave up reading. Writing checks became so frustrating that she was relieved when I offered to write checks, pay her bills, and balance her bank statement. In doing so I found she had paid many bills multiple times and at times she just filled out checks incorrectly.

One day, I noticed she had very little food in her refrigerator and when I took her to the grocery store, she was so disoriented that she left the store with only a few items. I started going to the store with her as often as I could to make sure she got enough food.

She became totally confused about taking her medications. She used eye drops for glaucoma, but her ophthalmologist told me that under the circumstances it would be best to stop the drops. That made one less thing to worry about.

My brother and I worked together to support mom and keep her safe and comfortable in her own home where she wanted to be. He lived nearby and would visit her daily, taking care of her yard and home maintenance. I lived 25 miles away and visited her several times a week. When her confusion and situation worsened, I started seeing her every day. It was getting to the point that we knew we were going to have to start looking for help, because we couldn't keep up the pace of meeting her increasing needs.

When my daughters visited, they saw the changes much more dramatically than we who were around her daily. Her neighbors were extremely helpful in sharing their observations of mother's condition. She still drove occasionally, but we realized this needed to stop, so we hid her car keys and drove her to where she needed to go. We both took her out for drives, out for a hamburger, whenever we could, to get her out of the house. Finally, I arranged for home care through a local agency and we had a caregiver visit once or twice daily to make sure she had a meal (which she gradually began to refuse), and to help her take her medication. My brother and I continued our daily visits.

We really needed to improve mom's nutrition. Since she no longer cooked for herself we arranged for 'Meals on Wheels.' In addition my brother picked up prepared foods at the store that she could easily heat and eat and we both provided meals from our own homes. She was not happy about the Meals on Wheels food and would usually throw most of it away. I found if I put the food on a plate and sat with her, she would eat it.

Fortunately before she became incompetent she updated her will and gave me Durable and Medical Power of Attorney authority to handle her affairs. We didn't know anything about dementia or Alzheimer's except all the myths and we didn't understand what was ahead for us. We tried to talk to mom about her condition and the need to plan for down the road. My brother had always been close to mom and he could get her to laugh and joke, but he couldn't get her to cooperate to discuss her situation. My efforts to talk with her about realities were fruitless. She didn't want to talk about it. She was OK – end of discussion. She could be quite stubborn. I guess I inherited some of her stubbornness, enough so that I had to take control and make decisions on her behalf. *Connie's story continues in Chapter 3.*

Donna's story

Donna had an easy time taking care of her husband for several years. She never considered herself as being a caregiver. In their years of marriage they had always taken care of each other and although he was having memory problems, taking care of him didn't require much more than she had always done for him. He was highly functional even with his dementia. People offered to help her, but she told them that she could manage. Donna's story begins when her world changed dramatically in a short period of time.

Howard had always been a quiet and soft-spoken man who enjoyed close friends and avoided crowds. That all began to change as he slipped deeper into dementia. He had been an easy keeper for several years.

Almost overnight, he didn't want to go out with friends. He had always been organized and neat and then he became disorganized and sloppy. He didn't seem to care about the messes he left for me to clean up. I'd get mad at him, but I just gritted my teeth and did all that I could to take care of him. He used to say, "Thank you" and now he mostly complains, no matter what I do for him. I just can't please him anymore and I feel like I'm a failure as a wife.

The biggest problem I ever faced was when he became incontinent. The frequency and intensity increased to the point I was cleaning up after him several times a day. I even bought a rug shampooer. Before long I was doing all the chores of bringing in the groceries, managing his medications, doing the yard work, taking care of the car, and other tasks that he had always done.

The most difficult and stressful task I had to do was our taxes. I had never done them before. The 24/7 workload, the stress, and not having any support was taking its toll. I felt exhausted and trapped. "Wear and Tear" described what was happening to my body and mind. My immune system couldn't keep up with all the bugs going around; I got sick and couldn't get enough sleep and I know I wasn't eating right.

I loved this man and he was drowning and I jumped in to save him and I was in over my head trying to save him and losing myself in the process. I felt doomed to failure no matter what I did. I was feeling more alone and getting desperate. I'm getting too old to be doing all this by myself. I knew I needed help but didn't know what I needed or what was even available. I heard about a support group and thought that maybe they could help me. *Donna's story continues in Chapter 3.*

Faye's story

Faye and her husband Jake retired and moved to a small mountain town in the Colorado Rocky Mountains. Except for a couple local stores they had to drive up to 60 miles to the nearest hospital, doctors, grocery store, and other amenities. Inconvenience taught newcomers to plan. They loved their small acreage where they could keep their horses and even had a beautiful stream flowing through the property. They were in heaven.

We were living the retirement life that we had saved and planned for all our married lives. About 15 years into living our dreams our world began to change. To make a long story short, Jake started having symptoms of Alzheimer's. At first he was just easily confused and was finding it difficult to concentrate, which led to his retirement. He couldn't do familiar tasks like writing a check or changing the oil in his truck. He wasn't driving as well and he had always been an exceptional driver. I knew something wasn't right but passed it off as his being absent-minded, forgetful, perhaps stubborn, or slowing down as part of the aging process.

I soon found myself doing more things that he had always done, but I easily picked up driving the tractor, stacking hay, and even did some minor repairs in the barn. In another year, however, he got worse and soon I no longer had time to ride my horse or play bridge with my friends. I didn't even have time to do chores, and our piece of heaven suffered from a lack of attention.

It seemed like each day or so there were new challenging behaviors. Jake started wandering and we didn't have neighbors living nearby to watch out for him. The land was uneven and rocky in places and he fell a couple times, but he used a walking stick and was able to get up. He began tossing most of his clothes out of his closet onto his bed or waking up several times each night and getting dressed thinking it was morning. He then got to the point where he couldn't speak clearly. I was getting stressed, exhausted and my health was deteriorating by all these things.

Jake agreed that we should get a doctor's evaluation. Friends of ours gave us the nave of a neurologist they preferred, who ordered an MRI and recommended further neuropsychological testing. The diagnosis was moderate to severe Alzheimer's disease. The news wasn't as much of a shock because I knew something was wrong, and now I had a name for it. A name is one thing but understanding was another ball game. Living with it was the hardest. *Faye's story continues in Chapter 3.*

Brenda's story

Brenda and Tom did everything together. He was successful in most all his endeavors, but he was always aware that it was his precious wife who encouraged him when he was down and rejoiced with him when he was successful. It didn't matter who was up or down, they were always there for each other. This relationship never changed when he would need her more than ever before.

From the first time I met Tom, when we were freshmen in college, he was always the gentleman: kind, considerate, and slow to anger. He was an avid sportsman but baseball was his favorite. He was extremely competitive but not to a fault, always fair. He was a great supporter of his vocation, his family and his friends. He retired early, for which I am thankful, and he hunted, fished, traveled, golfed, and played bridge, all with vigor.

We moved from our home in Minnesota to Western Colorado to be close to our kids.

Tom was still able to enjoy playing golf, but he let go of other activities he used to enjoy. I began to really notice his slow decline and if he ever feared what was coming and he never expressed it. The only thing that really bothered him was when he had to give up driving, and, I honestly believe that was when he gave up living. Tom loved to drive and we had gone on many marathon trips all over the country. He drove five days a week for much of his career.

His first signs of 'being different' was when he started forgetting how to do things, how to get from place to place, sitting around a lot, and asking questions I knew he knew the answer to. He was constantly repeating himself, was restless, and he lost interest in the activities he used to love.

I started doing more and more of the things he used to do. These changes were so obvious that all our kids were concerned. We had a family meeting and discussed the situation. We all knew his dad had died from what was thought to be Alzheimer's disease. So, we knew what had to be done and had the medical and financial papers drawn up.

His neurologist put him on some memory enhancing drugs, but they did not agree with him and he was taken off those after three months. From there he went into 'sundowning' every evening he wandered around the house and got disoriented.

Sometimes he got a vacant look in his eyes and just stared into space. He was always so easy going and then he became more easily agitated when I questioned him. He was restless and one night he packed his clothes, because he was going 'home'. He didn't recognize people he had known all his life and was becoming more belligerent if I insisted on his doing something. He had always taking good care of himself and then he quit taking showers, going to bed, or changing his clothes. Life was unraveling. *Brenda's story continues in Chapter 3.*

The Forest View

Through all the despair and grief, caregiving is a teacher and you are a good learner. You often don't understand what you have experienced and you certainly don't feel glad for the experience, but you learn anyway.

Even after caregivers have long suspected dementia, many families delay getting a diagnosis. A diagnosis can be helpful. An early diagnosis not only establishes medical and mental baselines, it also helps you begin to learn, plan, and adapt. When you learn enough to understand that the disease is going to kill your loved one and that you can't fix that, then you begin to accept reality; your job to make your loved one comfortable, not to make them well. An exam may determine there is no cause for alarm, because it may be normal aging or it's not serious and there is a simple fix.

Some caregivers reach out to family for understanding and support. It can be disappointing that children and others do not immediately offer the help you hoped for. Some may be threatened by the thought that their life is already out of control and helping you is too much to add. Every family has a strained relationship or two. The tendency to bring up past grievances can add to the emotional load. Some will offer help and not follow through, while others deny anything is wrong. "You must be exaggerating. Last time I saw mom she was fine."

You may be put off by a comment like, "Mom you know him better than anyone. You can do it." They don't know that mom is hiding her weaknesses. When family visits at Thanksgiving she responds with grace and joy, the family may not understand the struggles you deal with when they aren't around. They fall for her deception and as they leave someone says, "I don't know what you're complaining about." They don't know how hard you worked to get her ready, or what a mess you have to clean up afterwards. Their lack of understanding and support are heart wrenching.

Many families are dispersed across the country so driving or flying for hours makes visits less frequent and shorter. It can be difficult for new caregivers to acknowledge these barriers. Your family history influences how your parents cared for their siblings and parents. In turn, your parents influenced you approach caregiving. You may remember how your mom took care of her mom, so they are your role models. Our society has changed and the old role models may not fit your circumstances.

Emotional support, especially in the early stages, may even be more important than respite care. Frequent telephone, emails and texts lets you know they are thinking about you. You might find a caregiver support group a good place to share and be understood. Caregiver stress challenges our commitment throughout this journey. No matter how much we love someone the physical and mental toll manifests itself with insomnia, weight gain, elevated blood pressure, and frequent illnesses.

Alzheimer's and other neurological terminal diseases have been called 'the long goodbye' It is both long and goodbye. There are times when you think the end is imminent and then it goes on and on. Caregivers experience one loss after another. When the loved one, for the first time, puts on a blouse backwards or forgets to flush the toilet or can't remember how to make a favorite recipe, the caregiver grieves the loss. Some of these changes are barely noticeable and others create real emotional turmoil. The first time your husband wanders off and gets lost or falls, may create a crisis for you; "How do I deal with this? Do I have to quit work?" Goodbye means your loved one is leaving. Every time there is a leaving, there is grieving. Each loss triggers fear of the future and sadness for the disappearing past.

Mental and physical decline have periods of losing it and periods of finding it again. One day dad gets neatly groomed and dressed just fine and the next day he can't remember how to tie his shoes. The backward blouse may be on correctly tomorrow, the toilet may be flushed, and she may make a great meal tonight.

This rollercoaster of behavior and the gradual losses that occur over a long time create emotional turmoil. Sometimes you overreact, thinking the change is devastating, "I don't know if I can stand it any longer." Sometimes, when the loved one regains a memory or behavior you cling to the thought that all is okay. It might help to remind yourself that the good days won't last, and the bad days won't either.

Our dilemma has been called 'Ambiguous Loss'. Dad is himself sometimes and absent other times. The term fits. After a long time we get tired of grieving. In extreme cases we can even lose the capacity to care. 'Caregiver fatigue' or 'Caregiver burnout" is serious, because our own health can begin to fail and we might stop giving the care our loved one needs.

Your loved one is in a pit and you want to jump in and rescue him. All you accomplish by getting in the pit is that now you both need rescuing. Rather than jumping in, stay safely on the edge. You do this by taking care of yourself first. Maybe you can't get away from the stress for a day. Ask a neighbor to take him to lunch. Perhaps, seclude yourself for ten minutes. Perhaps you can mediate or pray. Just try to relax, breathe deeply and concentrate on not being a caregiver for just a few minutes.

Don't be too hard on yourself. If you expect to save your loved one from decline or death, you will fail. Learn to blame the disease not your loved one, not only for their deteriorating condition, but also for the adaptations you have to make for your own dreadful situation. No one can make this journey without becoming worn down. When you lose emotional control it is a signal that you have reached your limits. When it happens, blame your situation, blame the disease. Recognize you need a break and find help.

Talk to a counselor, a peer-coach or join a support group. Some caregivers take their loved one to adult day care. You might asked a loved one's friend to come be with him or her while you leave for a few hours. Taking care of yourself is the first step in being a good caregiver.

Every family member has his or her own relationships. Each has a relationship with others as well as with mom and dad. Everybody in the family has emotional baggage from their past that complicates decision-making when the time comes to address late in life planning.

There are resources for family conversations when there is animosity that prevents family dialogue. Siblings can be just as stubborn as their parents — wonder where they picked up on that? Each has a different perspective of what should be done to accommodate mom and dad, especially when one or both exhibit symptoms of dementia. Too often the one with dementia gets all the attention and consideration. It is important for all the important people to listen to each other without judging or trying to fix the past. It should be a time to talk honestly about individual feelings and work toward forgiving the past which doesn't necessarily mean forgetting. This is a time to clean out old mental filters that inhibit fresh thinking. The family may need new approaches to solve problems and to support the loved one and you. A family counselor can help bring you together to contribute positive ideas and solutions.

Chapter 3

Reach Out: I need help

Your caregiver burden goes up as your loved one′s ability to function goes down. It is easy for a caregiver to say, "I can handle this," when taking on everyday chores: fixing meals, cleaning the house, and shopping. The burden is bigger when it's necessary to help your loved one with things you aren't used to: bathing, dressing, using the toilet or even walking. It is especially challenging to care for a loved one of the opposite sex. The weight of all the rocks you add to your backpack wears you out and makes you realize you need help. When you begin sacrificing all your time, the stage is set for fatigue and you don't even know it.

The strong person says, "I can do it." The burdened person says, "I need help." The wise person finds help. Getting help early for your loved one is important for you both. Don't let saying to yourself, "I can handle this" lead to saying "I can do everything myself forever". The reality is that no one can care for another around the clock. Most caregivers at the end wish they had asked for help sooner.

Caregivers wrestle with guilt. Am I admitting defeat by asking for help? Do I need assistance for me or for my loved one? The answer is that you both need help. It isn't a matter of either-or. It is necessary for both of you to remain as healthy and energized as possible. That is why the flight attendant instruct us to put on our own oxygen mask first. If we don't take care of ourselves we may lose the ability to care for others.

When reality collides with fantasy reality wins. Caregivers hit a wall of physical limits, exhaustion, lack of sleep, and stress. We are frustrated and grieve the relentless decline of our loved one. Sooner or later we come to understand; we accept that the goal is to provide comfort for our loved one and keep our own sanity and health.

The diagnosis and prognosis of the disease has a lot to do with determining what kind of help you might need. There are different considerations for these maladies and yet common needs as well. Some may require special equipment, house modifications and other physical changes. Others may find that practical things like housekeeping, yard work, and day care are all that is needed. Getting help will lighten your backpack.

One of your greatest caregiver needs may be emotional support. You turn to family first, but most families have some strains. Some are so distant that they can't help as much as they would like. Some caregivers are alone and have no family or friends to help at all. Find a friend you trust and be candid about your challenges. Look for a caregiver support group to find others who feel like you do. Fortunately, many communities have resources for seniors and disabled citizens. It is up to you as the caregiver to find all the help you need.

Picture your life as a tire that has physical, mental, social, and spiritual needs. If one part of a tire leaks air, the ride becomes rough. Given enough time, it will wear out the suspension system. Likewise, the unbalanced caregiver can wear out. Look at yourself, "Are you out of round?"

Reaching out: I need help

Ted-Getting finances in order
Fred-Working with home care
June-Giving respite to my sister
Brenda-When the help failed
Charlotte-I've never been so alone
Linda-I had to take care of myself
Roger-The light at the end of the tunnel
Connie-Tag-teaming wasn't enough
Donna-I'd never done that before
The Forest View

Ted's story continues

Ted and Flo were living their dream retirement until she began to have trouble moving around and she just wasn't as sharp as she used to be. They went to their doctor and neurologist who gave them the diagnosis that Flo had a form of palsy that eventually would have symptoms of dementia. In its later stage, the disease progresses rapidly. Ted was beside himself grieving and feeling lost and wondering what to do.

I didn't know what to do next. We had another appointment with our neurologist. He gave me the name and phone number of a peer-coach whom he knew to be an experienced caregiver and who volunteers to come alongside of struggling caregivers like me. I called and we got together for coffee and I unloaded my grief on him. I found him to be the first person I had talked to who understood what I was going through. He listened, didn't try to fix me or tell me what to do, and encouraged me to start attending a caregiver support group.

I'll never forget the first time I went to my support group. At first I listened to other caregivers and although I didn't intend to say anything, I decided to share my story. I just got started and broke down and started crying. The lady sitting next to me reached over and squeezed my hand. A man across from me said, "I was sitting in your chair six months ago crying my eyes out. You're going to be okay. We're with you." My embarrassment left me immediately when I saw their tears of empathy.

I was overwhelmed by the group's compassion and understanding. Going to my support group became a bimonthly priority to drive 35 miles. They were my lifeline. I don't know how I'd have made it without them. They were the only support I had for a long time. My stepchildren never had much to do with me and when I told them about their mother's dementia, all I heard was, "The problem is with you, not with our mother."

Then one day my stepdaughter called and said she wanted to come see her mother. My coach told me to get out of the house and go fishing. Her daughter came and I left. When I came home at the end of the day (with a nice catch of trout), my stepdaughter met me at the door. "Dad (she had never called me dad), how do you live with this?" and "How can my brother and I help you." We cried and hugged each other.

I learned a lot about forgiving that day. Caregiving taught me tolerance and that led to patience and forgiveness. She could no longer deny the reality that I had told them about so many times. It took some experiential learning to understand what I was living with.

I listened to other caregivers in my support group and before long I got a lot of ideas to help me adapt to the ever-changing circumstances. I contacted our regional AAA Community Living Services and got some home-care assistance. I kind of felt guilty about getting help, but it didn't take long for me to appreciate someone else doing some housekeeping and being with Flo a few hours a week that gave me a little respite break as well.

It was becoming obvious that down the road I might need to place Flo into a nursing home. I could see our savings and investments going to a nursing home and leaving me out in the cold. I went to an attorney who specialized in estate planning and got my finances straightened out. I wish that I would have done a better job of financial planning years before, but I kept putting it off.

Although the home-care assistance was a tremendous help for a few hours each week, it was the early morning and late evening that were the worst. As soon as a caregiver left, Flo would start clinging to me. She was so scared and insecure and I was her security blanket. Even with the help, I was having those same feelings of being at the end of my rope. *Ted's story continues in Chapter 4.*

Fred's story continues

Fred was getting frustrated by his wife's behaviors and all the chores he was having to assume. He was having to learn housekeeping skills and other tasks that Bridget had always done. The caregiving role was getting to him. He was a positive person, but her constant negativity was dragging him down. He didn't know how to handle Bridget, let alone deal with his own feelings. He was a stubborn man who had always been a can-do, I-can-fix-it kind of guy, and this was something beyond his capabilities.

I did a poor job of letting others help me. Friends were nice to ask, but I didn't know what I needed, and anyway, I thought I could handle it. Partly it was pride and an emotional commitment to doing everything myself. After all, she was my wife; it was my responsibility to care for her. We had shared our lives, raised our son, helped each other through school, and built a successful business. Bridget's diagnosis at age 66 came out of the blue and upset our plans for the future way too early.

Now it was my time as the husband to take care of her. It's what our parents and family did. I guess I saw myself as a husband rather than a caregiver. It took a while for me to know that I needed help too, and how to let others into my life.

Housekeeping was new to me. One of the first things I noticed was the ring around the toilet bowl. I scrubbed and scrubbed but couldn't get rid of it. I went online and found a video on how to clean a toilet. So I went to the store and got the suggested items and sure enough, got rid of the stain. I felt so proud of myself and shared it with our support group. The ladies got a real hoot picturing me on my knees cleaning a toilet.

After that I swallowed my pride and hired some homecare assistance. I assumed that the company who sent the help had people I could just turn loose. Rather, I had to spent time showing them what I wanted done and where the supplies were to do the job. They all did a good job after I told them what I expected. Bridget never liked my having help. I told her the help was for me so I could take better care of her. When the ladies arrived she often went to her room until they finished their work.

At first, I wanted to learn everything I could about the disease. What caused it? What is the prognosis? How will it change her life? How will it change my life? The answers were not hopeful. Life expectancy after diagnosis was 4-20 years, and I was 67 at the time. I imagined the worst: she would decline and I would go down with her. The more I thought about it, the more alone I felt.

I shared my dilemma with a concerned neighbor and she did the most graceful and important thing in my life since Bridget's diagnosis. She told me she had a friend in her church that seemed to be going through similar circumstances. She asked if I would like to meet him. We met for coffee and have continued to meet every week since then. He was wise and kind and above all else was a long-time caregiver. He understood my feelings and let me express mine without judging me.

I also found support groups for caregivers. The range of long-term illnesses and the challenges and small victories were as varied as the loved ones and the caregivers themselves. I always felt a lift and encouraged after sharing how hard caregiving was for me and how each meeting helped me adapt. We really did support each other.

It wasn't until much later in my journey that I even thought I would have a future. I once again had friends and interests while I was caregiving. I gave no thought to my life after Bridget's death. That was not a pleasant thought and I was afraid of the unknown.

I so missed the companionship of a woman and yet I was not interested in an adulterous affair. Just a woman I could talk to and hang out with would be enough. I didn't even feel good about having these thoughts while Bridget was very much alive.

I went to a licensed clinical social worker to get counseling, but we didn't talk about dating. We talked about the burdens of caregiving and what I had learned about myself along the way. This experience was changing me and I was finding strength to continue.

It was a long time, maybe two years after diagnosis, that I wanted to be kind to myself and wanted to engage with the world in small ways. That let me appreciate when neighbors asked to take Bridget to lunch and let me go hit golf balls for an hour. My son provided great comfort by coming over on short notice when I felt blue or was about to lose patience. A few friends invited me to neighborhood potlucks. Those gatherings were awkward for me and I often went home frustrated, but I appreciated the invitations.

Bridget's condition continued downward. I had thought I could take care of her for a long time, but things were beginning to get me down even though I had some help. *Fred's story continues in Chapter 4.*

June's story

June's sister had been taking care of their mom for several years and the stress was taking a toll on her and her marriage. June hadn't seen her mom for two years and during that time dementia was changing their mother. June went back to relieve her sister and was looking forward to some good times and having fun with her mom.

Sis met me at the airport and tried to tell me that mom had gone downhill. I just couldn't picture mom in such a state. Sis had told me that we needed to place mom into a nursing home and the very thought of doing that made me mad. Surely she was exaggerating and just needed a little break. Mom couldn't be that bad off since the last time I had seen her. I was in total denial.

When I walked into the house, mom just looked at me with a "Who are you?" kind of look. She didn't recognize me. I said, "I'm June." She replied, "I have a daughter by that name." My own mother didn't know me. I started to cry. Sis put her arm around me and told mom, "This IS your daughter June." Mom said, "Oh, Hi." I gave her a hug, but she didn't hug me back. The reality of what Sis had been telling me hit me like a ton of bricks. I excused myself and wept.

Sis and her husband left for a vacation and I soon got into the routine of caring for mom. I was alarmed that she had changed so much. I had to walk her to the bathroom and helped her use the toilet. She didn't want to shower and I finally had to get into the shower with her. I gave up trying to bathe her every day. I had to help her dress, comb her hair (which I loved to do) and helped brush her teeth.

One day she fell out of her chair and I could barely get her up off the floor. I cooked her favorite meal but I couldn't get her to eat it. She had always enjoyed my cooking and her rejecting it made me feel like a failure. I had to walk beside her wherever she went because she could barely shuffle and I was afraid that she would fall.

What really drove me nuts were the times when she would ask me a question and I'd answer. Then, two minutes later she would ask the same question and I'd answer again. This would go on and on and I'd get to the point that I yelled at her and told her I'd already answered her question. She would withdraw from me in fear. She'd stop for a while and then it would start all over again, maybe with a question or repeating what she had just said. I got so frustrated and angry and I'd say just about anything to get her to shut up. My anxiety was off the chart. On top of all that, she kept asking, "Who are you?" I could tell my blood pressure was rising and I was not a happy camper. I was counting the days until Sis returned.

Mom took a lot of naps and I was so worn out that I took some, too. When she was awake she wandered around the house. Once, when I wasn't watching, she walked out onto the street, but a neighbor saw her and walked her back to the house. After that I wouldn't take my eyes off her.

I felt totally inept to perform my caregiver role. On top of all that, I knew I was in this for the long haul, for however many years that would be. My brother was slower to react to the changes; he was so conflicted about her condition that he at times dreaded and avoided the decisions and actions needed. I know his concern and worry was as agonizing as mine.

Mom started wandering out of the house and she was no longer safe in her own home, especially at night. It became obvious to me that we needed to place mom into a care facility. My brother wanted her to move in and live with him. He fixed up a bedroom and I agreed to that on a trial basis. After mom had lived there for three weeks I knew that we could not provide the level of care she needed. My brother was totally stressed caring for her. I began visiting different care facilities, but my brother was so adamant about keeping her in his home that he wouldn't go with me to visit care facilities. We must both have inherited our mother's stubbornness; however, I knew we could no longer take care of mom at home. *June's story continues in Chapter 4.*

Brenda's story continues

Tom was getting more difficult for Brenda to manage. She was getting frustrated that she couldn't get him to take care of himself. He didn't want to shower and he became sloppy in the way he dressed. She watched the man she loved become more and more a shell of what he had been. He was moving slowly but still loved to go for walks. It was this favorite past time that led to a "Silver Alert".

As Tom's dementia increased it became clear that I could not take care of him 24/7. Our kids kept after me to hire somebody to clean the house to ease my burden. I resisted their pressure, because I was physically able to take care of Tom and the house.

The burden increased to the point that I eventually gave in and hired a housekeeper. It didn't take long and I was glad to have the help. I was spending most of my time taking care of Tom and not taking care of myself all that well. So, I enrolled him in a daycare program. Having him in day care was a great relief to me as it gave me time to do everyday chores and have some quiet time for myself. He adapted very well and enjoyed his time there.

One of the most alarming phone calls I ever had however, was the day the owner of the day-care facility called. Tom had somehow gotten out of the house and they could not find him. The daycare was in a residential area, on a dead-end street with a golf course behind it. They figured he had been gone only a few minutes, but just as anyone with Alzheimer's, he was like a child and could slip away in the blink of an eye. I immediately called my son and told him that dad had escaped!

When I arrived at the day care, several police cars and emergency vehicles were on the scene. I started driving up and down every street in the subdivision looking for him. This went on for another half hour and no sign of Tom. I saw everyone running toward the house, so I figured he had been found. But to my horror a white SUV, same color and size as mine, with the keys in it, was missing. It was agreed that the car and Tom had been missing at least an hour and a half. By now our son was there and we started driving all over looking for the white SUV.

The Colorado State Patrol put out a Silver Alert bulletin that was posted to all police and Highway Patrol Troopers within in a 100-mile radius of the city. There were lots of people who knew Tom, heard the alert, and were out looking for him. I went home, in the hopes that he might have gone there. As afternoon faded I was panic-stricken, because I was so afraid he would not only hurt of kill himself but some innocent person as well.

I was at wits´ end when I got the call from the police department that Tom had been found in Durango, Colorado. Tom hadn't driven a car in three years. He had driven 100 miles on the San Juan Scenic Byway and over one of the most dangerous highways in Colorado, including three high mountain passes. This narrow two-lane highway is known for its many switchbacks, lack of guard rails, vertical drop offs, and is a challenging drive for even a sober driver, let alone someone with Alzheimer's disease.

When Tom arrived in Durango, he stopped at an automobile dealership on the outskirts of town. When a salesman approached him, he could not tell him his name or where he was from. The salesman immediately called the police. An officer recognized the situation from the Silver Alert and took Tom to McDonald´s for a burger and on to the police station.

We left immediately to pick him up. I can never say enough good about our law enforcement agencies and thank them for their fierce search and rescue of Tom. When I saw Tom, he looked up at me with a big smile on his face and said "HI." As if this was just another day in the life of a caregiver and her loved one!

When I think of all the horrible ways this trip could have ended and that he was able to drive and the fact that he didn't hurt himself, or wind up in New Mexico, Arizona, or over a cliff off Red Mountain Pass, I know there had to be a guardian angel riding on his shoulder, praying for backup.

I knew then that sooner or later I was going to have to place Tom into a care facility, but that was a long way off in the future - I thought! *Brenda's story continues in Chapter 4.*

Charlotte's story continues

Charlotte's husband had only few observable symptoms of Parkinson's disease in its early stage, but he soon had problems with getting around, falling, swallowing, tremors, and memory loss. He was difficult for Charlotte to manage. He became belligerent and wouldn't cooperate and yet he was totally dependent on her. He was angry because he couldn't function like he used to, and he took his frustration out on Charlotte. She was becoming desperate for help, overwhelmed with being alone. Laying her pride aside she wisely reached out for help.

I didn't know how to start looking for help. I hadn't given any thought to what help I could use. A friend told me that she found some help from the Area Agency on Aging (AAA) so I contacted them. The options counselor came to our home and evaluated it for safety and Carl's condition. She helped us find a reliable home-care assistance company. The ladies who came to our home were caring and professional. Their visits allowed me to leave the house without worrying about his safety. When the caregiver was watching him, I was able to visit with friends or play tennis. That really helped reduce my stress level so that I could face the challenges at home.

Our friends offered to help, but I was afraid that my Carl would become combative in my absence. I didn't want just anyone coming into our house to take care of him, because they wouldn't have known how to handle his behavior. Even though I was rarely able to accept help from them, just knowing that they were willing to help was comforting.

Carl's Parkinson's got worse and he needed help showering and dressing, I felt emotionally and physically drained, because it took a lot of effort to help him. I think he was embarrassed that he needed help with even simple tasks. He would resist my help and get mad at me. At times I just felt like throwing up my hands and giving up.

In addition to taking care of Carl, I took over doing the yard work that he had always done. It didn't take long before I realized that I couldn't do it all and hired a landscaper to do the mowing and other outside chores. I was very fortunate to be able to hire help.

Once I was sharing my frustrations with one of our home caregivers who had been with us for some time. She said to me, "Carl isn't Carl anymore so you can't expect him to act like he used to." Those words sunk in. and I felt like I was in a living funeral that wouldn't end. He was physically in front of me and yet, he wasn't there.

Ever so slowly I lost my sense of freedom and peace of mind. It didn't matter if I was at home or away (with someone watching him), he was always on my mind. My entire day and life revolved around his needs to the point that I neglected my own. I was stressed and anxious about the future in addition to being physically worn out.

I lived in fear of losing my future. I was so saddened to see him struggle, knowing that it was only going to get worse. I started having thoughts that I wished he would pass away. Then I'd be conflicted in my mind whether I was just thinking about myself or his being free from this dreaded disease.

I attended a Parkinson's support group. The guest speakers and some attendees' responses were informative in terms of understanding the disease. That information was sometimes overwhelming and depressing but helpful. The focus on guest speakers left little time to share experiences or offer support within the group.

Later, I joined a caregiver support group which focused on giving emotional support regardless of the disease or infirmity. Associating with other caregivers who shared their experiences helped fill a void. They helped me deal with the emotions and caregiver stress and became essential to my well-being. The caregiver meetings were a safe place to share my journey, be supported by others, and in turn offer support to those in the group who expressed their needs. I found that even my very close friends were unable to understand what I was going through. As a result, if it weren't for my caregiver support group, I would have felt very alone. They got me through some difficult times.

Carl was the love of my life and I hated what Parkinson’s was doing to him. In his late stage he couldn’t follow a conversation and just stared into space while pretending to watch TV. During his last few days at home, he fell several times and I had to call 911 for help since I couldn´t lift him on my own.

Looking back, I wish that I would have had a better idea of what to expect with Parkinson’s and more guidance as to its progression, even though. I know that the symptoms are different for each patient. Each day brought new challenges that I had to find a way to handle without having the tools to do what was best for him and at the same time take care of myself. *Charlotte’s story continues in Chapter 4.*

Linda’s story continues

Linda committed to be her mother’s caregiver. She sacrificed her own well-being to give all her attention to her mother. Linda had no knowledge of dementia and had no idea how to cope and, even less, how to take care of herself.

On the one hand, my brother and his wife were angry with me for moving mother to my home, but on the other hand they didn't want to be involved with her day-to-day care. The other family members were happy for her moving in with me and thought it was a good idea.

I managed her medications and took her to her doctor appointments. When she needed hearing aids, I helped her get them. I took over all her financial affairs, paid her bills, filed taxes and maintained her insurance policies. I was frustrated and exhausted. It was overwhelming to take care of mom on top of managing my own affairs.

I was consumed with taking care of her and gave up my personal time. It made me sad and angry that I didn't have any time to myself. After quite a while, I realized that I needed to make time for myself and looked for ways to do that, so I joined the gym, I did have some good laughs and lighter times there, but mostly I was just trying to stay on top of everything.

I wish I would have known the prognosis of her condition before I took on the role as her caregiver. I had no idea what was ahead for me. If my brother and I had gotten together earlier and gotten a diagnosis we could have made better decisions regarding her future care. I don't think the average doctor or therapist has much insight to help caregivers cope with their new role. I would have wanted the doctors to be more sympathetic and helpful, but they were not.

Linda's story continues in Chapter 4.

Roger's story continues

Betty Jo's dementia took over their lives. Roger didn't know how to handle her hallucinations and other behaviors. He tried everything to restore her to reality. That just made things worse, because he didn't understand what was happening to her or to himself. He had few coping skills and was suffering from compassion fatigue, which was dragging him down. He needed help and fast.

I was having coffee with some friends, one of whom was a professional counselor. I told him I was falling apart and needed his help. He told me. "I don't fix people, but I will walk alongside of you and point things out in the forest that you don't see, because of all those trees." He had been a caregiver for his parents and he understood beyond his formal education what a caregiver goes through. I needed someone who understood and with whom I could confide my feelings as I walked up that forested road.

Several years passed before Betty Jo's psychiatrist used the word "dementia". I was never given an explanation of what that word and all its ramifications meant. It would be years of going to caregiver workshops, seminars and reading until I would gain some understanding of terms like Alzheimer's and dementia. I learned that it was important to understand the prognosis of any disease and what to expect, but regardless, it was the behaviors that I had to live with and not definitions.

I read many books having to do with Alzheimer's, but few helped me cope with what was going on at home. Only through my counselor and later my caregiver support group did I find the emotional support that got me through the next 16 years of caregiving. Information and resources are helpful, they really are, but they didn't help all that much with my emotions.

Betty Jo loved to drive, but one day I was riding with her and realized that her reactions were too slow and she asked me several times where we were going. I told her that I thought she shouldn't be driving and that I would be so honored to be her chauffeur. I wanted to minimize Betty Jo's fear of losing her driving privileges. She accepted my offer and never drove again.

My own mother had lived in a small town with no public transportation. She failed the renewal driving test five times before the DMV refused her a license. The neighbors, police and family rejoiced that she could no longer drive. No thought was given to the turmoil she now faced. Becoming dependent on others was traumatic for a senior citizen such as her, who had lived independently all her life. The loss of her driving privilege was really the loss of her independence and it lessened her ability to take care of herself.

Betty Jo slipped deeper into her dementia. She lived in a world of hallucinations. At first I tried to reason with her and bring her back to reality - my reality. I kept trying to fix her.

Then one day she walked into the room and asked, "Did you see the little black dog run through the living room?"

I answered, "We've never had a black dog." That started an argument every time she "saw" the dog. I began using validation techniques that I had learned at a validation seminar taught by Naomi Feil, a renowned authority on how to communicate with the demented.

Another day, when Betty Jo asked, "Did you see the little black dog?" I put my new training to the test as I stepped into her world.

I answered, "You really love that dog, don't you?"

"Yes," she answered.

I asked, "What´s its name?"

She answered, "Blackie."

"Did you play with it?" I asked

She answered, "Yes, and I made dresses for it."

I walked onto the patio and called out into the darkness, "Here Blackie." I assured her that Blackie was out for a run and was okay and would be right back. She relaxed knowing I cared.

I wondered where that all came from, so I called my stepson and told him. He shared how as an only child, she grew up at the edge of a small town, and only had one playmate - you guessed it, a little dog named "Blackie." Perhaps her brain was recalling how that little dog made her feel when she was a little girl and she wanted that feeling back. I learned through training and experience that I had to step outside of myself, take a few deep breaths, and enter her world.

Trying to restore her memory was impossible. Only I was the one who could change. I learned that the behavior was seldom the issue, but that her feelings were usually the source of a behavior. That dog gave her feelings that she could remember. As soon as I learned this, life smoothed out a little, be it ever so briefly, before the next hallucination came out of nowhere.

As her short-term memory failed, she would ask the same question or make the same statement again and again. It liked to have driven me crazy answering her. I asked my counselor for advice and he gave me a few ideas to try. I changed the subject, reflected her comments, and sometimes I just excused myself and went into another room, hoping she would forget.

Betty Jo began wandering around the house day and night. One of the men in our support group suggested I install burglar alarms on the doors. I bought a set. When the door opened, a loud and shrill alarm sounded. But things didn't work out the way I thought. The very first time she opened the door and the alarm went off, she closed the door and then opened it again. Pretty soon she was mesmerized by her ability to make music. I uninstalled them.

Next, I contacted the police department that furnished radio direction finders for at-risk people. Betty Jo thought it was an ugly bracelet but wore it anyway. One day she wandered off and I called the police department and an officer tracked her down and escorted her back to the house. But she wouldn't come inside because, "That strange man is in my house." After an hour of trying to convince her that I was her husband, the officer called our sons, but even they couldn't convince her. Finally, the officer had me drive off and they got her into the house. I returned and the officer convinced her to let me sleep in the guest bed again.

On my next visit, my counselor asked, "Do you feel trapped?" I answered, "Yes, I'd have to jump up to touch bottom." He said, "That is because you see no way out and the only way out is to get help." Seeing my desperation, he told me to go to our county Health and Human Services office to check into enrolling Betty Jo into Medicaid.

We're neither rich nor poor, but the cost of nursing home care would bankrupt us in just a few months. I went to an attorney who worked us through the hoops to get Betty Jo enrolled with Medicaid. For five years I had been living in that caregiver vortex sucking me down into a never-ending dilemma of caring for her at home by myself. When she was accepted into Medicaid, we were eligible to get some home-care assistance, which really helped me.

Then one day the social worker told me about the Program for All-inclusive Care of the Elderly (PACE) that had just opened in our county. As soon as she was accepted into the PACE program, she went to adult day care five days a week and that gave me respite time to take care of myself at least for a few hours during the week. Even with time to do what I wanted, the stress was killing me. She was always on my mind. I don't know how I would have gotten this far without my counselor. I just needed someone to talk to who understood what I was going through. I didn't need a pity party; I was only wanting to find solutions – and not remain in such a depressed state.

I started journaling and I wrote daily about what Betty Jo did and how I was coping and feeling. After a few years I looked back and I had documented what I called my Tempestuous Journey. I know other caregivers who journal and document the behaviors of a loved one. Doing so can be of great value to show to a doctor, an attorney or even a judge. It gives written evidence of the deteriorating condition of a loved one needing more care and what you have gone through as the caregiver.

At about the five-year mark of my caregiver journey, I was battling depression. I just wanted to mope around doing nothing. My counselor contacted my doctor and suggested he prescribe an anti-depressant. The stress was getting to me. He also contacted PACE and recommended that they provide me a few days of respite. I was so surprised to get just a few days in which Betty Jo was in a care facility and I didn't have to worry about her well-being. Yet, she was still on my mind, but casting a fly, catching fish, and being in the mountains got my mind cleared for a while.

Betty Jo enjoyed the day-care activities. I had regular care conferences with the PACE staff. Our social worker told me that Betty Jo was doing well at the Senior Community Care Center. I responded, "That's wonderful to hear." As the late radio broadcaster Paul Harvey asked, "Do you want to hear `the rest of the story'?"

I had four major surgeries in one year. My stress had exacerbated existing physical weaknesses. The last surgery went sour and I was in and out of the hospital and nursing home rehabilitation center for two months. During that time Betty Jo was placed into respite care in the same nursing home. We could have meals together and see each other. When I got out of the hospital, and Betty Jo from respite care, things really "went south" in a hurry. I was in for another wild rollercoaster ride.

"It ain't that rosy at home." I told our social worker about the turmoil that I was living in and he listened, but he did nothing but encourage me to "hang in there." If things got any worse, hanging t could be an option to escape. I didn't see it coming, but a life-changing event was about to happen in just two days. *Roger's story continues in Chapter 4.*

Donna's story continues

Even though Donna's husband was in the early stage of dementia, he was able to do many of the things he had always done. Before long however, he was forgetting how to do familiar tasks. He couldn't learn new things. Donna began taking on more and more chores. All the while she saw him losing his short-term memory and judgement to the point that he couldn't make sound decisions. The caregiver burden began to weigh Donna down. Aging takes a toll on a caregiver's strength and endurance. Adult children may not realize that mother isn't the same strong woman who raised them. The additional responsibilities were wearing Donna down to the point where she admitted that she needed help.

Someone in my support group said that she got some help from the AAA. I made an appointment with the options counselor who helped me find adult daycare. Howard enjoyed his time there, and they dealt with his incontinence. I began to get a little time for myself. I planned my schedule to go to my caregiver support group where I found the emotional support I needed. They shared some ideas that had worked for them and I learned to try what worked for me. We shared our stories, and we laughed and cried together. We were family to each other. It was fun to share and to encourage one another to hang in there when the going was tough.

I knew that someday I would not be able to keep up the pace of being Howard's caregiver and would have to place him into a skilled nursing home. The financial burden would be overwhelming, but I was near the end of my rope. I went to an attorney to get help us with financial planning. He told me that we were too late to save all the assets we had worked so hard to accumulate for our retirement years. I could see that most of our assets would be going to a nursing home and I hated the thought of putting him there, but if his condition got much worse I wouldn't have any alternative. *Donna's story continues in Chapter 4.*

The Forest View

When our loved ones get to the point that it is unsafe to drive, families are faced with a difficult situation. In our society a driver's license means independence and liberty. When your loved one loses the right to drive they feel diminished.

Failure to take action to protect a loved one and the public can have tragic outcomes. We read reports of elderly people with dementia who go missing. Some are found alive, some die in crashes, others get lost. What is a family to do? Caregivers are creative to find solutions. Some contact the local police or sheriff's department to expressing their concern. Officers can request that the Department of Motor Vehicles retest their vision, knowledge and driving ability. Doctors can also make such requests. Loved ones sometimes respond to authority figures, even as they fight you. Caregivers have done everything from hiding the car keys, disconnecting ignition wires, and making up excuses for the car not running.

This is one of many life changes you face as your loved one's brain deteriorates. The traditional family roles change. You become more like a parent. But adults don't like being parented and you don't like to parent a parent or spouse.

Every caregiver is reluctant to seek help. The sooner you realize that this caregiving job is going to get more difficult, the sooner you will seek help. An expectation that our loved one will get better, or will stay the way they are, is not realistic. The hard-reality is that we must accept that this disease is going to kill our loved one. You might prolong life, you might make them more comfortable, but you can't stop the disease.

Yes, you are angry, that's part of grieving. You feel like you are raising a child when he or she becomes incontinent, unable to dress, or bathe. You become impatient. Impatience and anger are often signs that you are tired and overwhelmed. You are not failing. Your loved one is not at fault. You are in a very difficult situation and need help. Don't blame the patient, blame the disease. You might try thinking like this, "I am just a caregiver and I'm not going to act like a spouse." It might reduce your stress.

Professional caregivers try not to care too much. They try to leave their stress at work. They go home at night to be with their families and decompress. However, when professionals care for a family member, they can't leave the stress at home. Family caregivers have little or no respite, but we can try to be a little more like professionals and find a little relief and personal time to recharge. We can help our loved ones be comfortable and enjoy what they can, and we can try to ignore the rest.

Our expectations must change. We don't expect them to perform or react as they did before the onset of this mind-robbing disease. These changed views of your relationship help you see that your loved one as already partly gone, so you can more easily care out of love for the part that is still there.

Many caregivers and their loved ones share a strong and intimate relationship. As the disease progresses your intimacy diminishes and can be lost entirely. The loss is likely profound. It increases your feelings of isolation and loneliness. Your grief, while your loved one is alive and after death, is due to loss of both emotional and physical intimacy.

Your shared emotional experiences are important. You miss the meaningful conversations. They are a central part of who you are and how you see the world. The loss of intimacy means you lose the memories of laughing at silly things you did together, remembering the scary things you survived, and the secrets no one else knows.

The loss of emotional intimacy with a parent is why we all grieve for them. When they are gone they can't tell us about our past, give us their wisdom, or praise our successes. There is also a loss of non-sexual physical intimacy: their hugs, their smell, the texture of their skin, their voice, their laugh. This loss is often greater for an opposite sex parent.

Loss of intimacy for a spouse is clearly important. The deterioration of memory, appearance and function is great, and you grieve that loss. Appearance and touch have sexual meaning as well. The loss of sexual activity for a lover lying next to you at night magnifies your grief for touch and release.

Our stories do not discuss sexual intimacy often, perhaps because of taboos about acting on your needs while your loved one is still alive. Some may deny the need for intimacy or pretend it isn't important. Some may seek another partner. Please, acknowledge your feelings. It will help you understand what is happening and help you make good choices. The desire for intimacy, no matter what form it takes, is a natural part of who you are.

Caregiving is very lonely, so it is important to put together a support team. Your team may include family, friends, doctors, therapists, a pastor or spiritual leader, counselor, peer-coach, support group, a maintenance person, auto mechanic, tax consultant—whoever you need. These are the people you rely on. You may be unable to oversee medications while you are gone for a few hours. So you learn to rely on your team. Everyone's contribution is important to the goal of providing care for you and your loved one.

Go to your loved one's appointments so you can ask questions and discuss health issues. People with some types of dementia may not be able to answer correctly. You need to be there to give the doctor your observations and ask your questions. A loved one can fool a doctor and he or she needs to hear from you what is really going on. You need to know what the doctor says as well. Physicians and other providers must know what you can and can't do to provide care. You might make an appointment alone with your loved one's doctor to talk confidentially about your loved one and what you need.

Your own doctor is a key member of your support team. Have you told your doctor about your stress? Part of taking care of yourself is being physically, mentally, and spiritually fit.

When you go for a doctor appointment, take a list of questions and concerns. If you communicate the things on your mind, the time will be more profitable for you and your doctor. Many report insomnia, stress, depression and other physical ailments. Reach out for support and encouragement from your doctors and other health care providers. They need to know your limitations.

You can help by listening to the doctor's orders and see that they are carried out. You can update him or her about potential barriers. Remember: You are an important team member and good teams communicate.

To develop trust, understand some of the limitations of physicians: because of scheduling, they may not have the time to address all your issues in one appointment. They are mostly paid to provide care to the patient. They are not social workers. They can refer you to a counselor, a support group or a peer coach to help you learn the art and skill of caregiving. Doctors are frustrated with fatal diseases; they have few treatment options and wish they could offer hope.

Chapter 4

Delegate: We need professional help

Caregivers learn in the 'reaching out for help' phase that no caregiver can do it all forever. As the disease progresses your loved one needs more and more help. We learn to reach out for help to survive and to help our loved ones live comfortably. The time may come when you can't provide a safe environment and an acceptable level of care. You may be wearing out. The heavy caregiver burden of managing special needs, medications, coping with behaviors, and monitoring around the clock can become overwhelming. The time comes to give your backpack to someone else.

You want to provide care at home for as long as possible. Your loved one is happier and that makes you feel good, but when home care is neither safe nor practical it's time to consider other options. You may feel guilty. Some feel guilty for even thinking about placing a loved one. You may believe he or she will never agree to go.

You may find some comfort in the fact that you might not have to make the decision! It might fall into your lap. Your loved one may have a fall or some traumatic event that requires skilled nursing. A doctor may determine that home care is no longer adequate and recommends placement. The hospital team may require rehabilitation that can lead to placement.

Eventually, most loved ones need professional care. Sometimes a doctor directs care to be administered by nurses, CNAs, and therapists to provide services: injections, medicine management, bathing, dressing, and monitoring vital signs. In some cases, specialized equipment is necessary.

Long-term placement in a skilled nursing home is a major step. Mom may have said long ago, "I want to die in my home. Promise me that you'll never ever put me in a nursing home." The idea of placement sounds risky. The history of nursing homes is replete with bad press about over-medication and the abuse of seniors. Covid-19 has changed the way we think of safety for seniors in confined spaces. Only a few generations ago it was a cultural imperative to care at home. That feeling is still with us, but the long journey of caregiving today makes placement much more common.

Delegate: We need professional help

Ted-I found the help I needed
Dwight-Overload-help!
Fred-It was happening faster than I thought
Brenda-It fell into my lap
Charlotte-I resisted getting help
Linda-If only I'd known sooner
Roger-They saved me
Bill-Kidnapped!
Donna-I felt guilty about asking for help
Faye-Then it happened
Juanita-I didn't need help and died trying
The Forest View

Ted's story continues

At first Ted could handle it. With only a few added tasks, his caregiver burden wasn't all that difficult to carry, but then his situation progressed to the point that he wisely sought help. Even with more help that gave him some relief, his circumstances brought him to the realization that Flo wasn't going to get better and he couldn't continue trying to help her. He knew she was slowly dying and he wasn't going to be able to change the inevitable outcome of death. He decided it was time to act.

Flo's form of dementia progressed more rapidly than others. I had already taken advantage of home care and I was coping well. I regularly drove 35 miles to attend my support group. I needed them - and before long I learned that others benefited from my sharing what I was going through.

I knew that it might not be long before I would have to place Flo into a skilled nursing home. I visited the nursing homes in our area. I chose to enroll her into the PACE program in our county. We are fortunate to have one of the few rural PACEs in the country. The program enabled me to take care of her at home for a while longer. I was so glad that I had done some financial planning, even though it was too late to save all our assets.

I met with the PACE activity director, completed a questionnaire about Flo's background and interests, her fears, and skills. She got to know Flo and found things that she could do. At least when she was in day care, Flo did well and she started feeling better about herself. But that social structure wasn't present at home.

While Flo went to adult day care she got used to being in the nursing home setting, eating lunch, and socializing. She had been reluctant to go at first, but after the first week she was motivated to be with her new friends, who became like family to both of us. I had regular conferences with the staff to listen to their perspectives about Flo's declining condition and I shared with them how difficult it was getting for me to take care of her on weekends.

I began to wonder what Flo was going through. She seemed bored. Maybe that was because she couldn't remember things she used to enjoy, like reading and knitting. She had also been good at creating stuffed dolls for children but had lost the dexterity in her hands. Perhaps that is where some of her anger and feeling of worthlessness came from.

There were days when I got so sad that I just sat and didn't feel like doing anything. Then I decided I wasn't being myself anymore. I had to change. I was actually coping really well and had a lot going for both Flo and me. When she was in day care I occasionally made time to play a round of golf. I started getting more exercise and lost some weight. It felt good to have a little bit of freedom to do some of the things that I enjoy. Other things that I wanted to do would have to wait: our new RV had been sitting in the back lot for two years and I wondered if I would ever travel again. *Ted's story continues in Chapter 5.*

Dwight's story continues

Dwight's siblings had been taking care of their mother for several years. As dementia began to set in, however, they backed off. Dwight committed to be her long-term caregiver at the time their mother's dementia and health was getting worse. He lovingly provided the care she needed.

Mom was having the worst anxiety attack I had ever witnessed. She was thrashing around and screaming. I couldn't settle her down. In a panic myself, I called the doctor and then the ambulance. As it turned out, her body had stopped metabolizing the medicine and it was bringing on the attacks.

The emergency room doctor must have seen something in my face that told him I was in a crisis and he asked how I was holding up. For the first time I finally admitted that I was in rough shape. The first person I called once mom was in her room was my coach. He was the only one that I knew who understood what I was going through and he threw me a "lifeline". I let him know what had happened. He listened and validated my feelings and gave me the emotional support I needed to get through the next few days. It wasn't so much what he said, but the calming presence, even over the phone, of a friend meant so much then.

The doctor gave orders to have mom monitored and gradually reduced the medicine that was causing some of her increased anxiety. He started a different medication that she could tolerate and it helped keep her calm. I was relieved and looked forward to the day I would get to bring her home, but for how long I didn't know.
Dwight's story continues in Chapter 5.

Fred's story continues

Fred learned all he could about his wife's dementia. He tried to take care of himself by playing a round of golf now and then, and regularly attending a support group. He was watching his wife slowly die, but he hung in there and using local resources to give her the best care possible. He was committed and planned to take care of her for years to come.

Bridget got to where she didn't like to leave the house because of the anxiety and fear of embarrassing herself by not remembering names. She didn't want to see a doctor. When her anti-anxiety prescription ran low, she agreed to see a neurologist for a refill. She tolerated him, but when she needed the next refill, he was unavailable. To get a refill she agreed to see my family physician. He is a fine doctor and is interested in end-of-life care and is also the medical director of a nursing home that has an excellent memory care unit.

I updated him about Bridget's declining condition every time I had an appointment. When I took Bridget in to get the refill, he skillfully engaged her in conversation. I thought it went well. As I was leaving, he touched me on the shoulder and whispered to me, "Fred, you can have hospice support anytime you want it."

I was shocked to the core. I had no idea that she had declined enough to be eligible for hospice. I thought that hospice was available only if the patient was likely to die within six months. I never imagined that her death could be that close. She didn't seem that far gone.

All the way home my head was spinning. What did he see that I missed? I made an appointment to find out. He told me her dementia was advancing, but his immediate concern was her weight. She had gone from her normal 135 pounds down to 85 and she could not survive on her current diet. It was true she ate very little and mostly sweets and salty junk food. I couldn't get her to eat a healthy diet.

I asked him, "When you said I could have hospice, was that for me or for Bridget?"

He answered, "Both." I learned that was the mission of hospice.

I thought placement in a nursing home was down the road. It really did sneak up on me. As they say, "Sometimes it just falls in your lap." I knew down deep that I couldn't care for Bridget much longer. Although the doctor's assessment was unexpected, I realized it was a blessing and since the doctor wanted it for her, I had less guilt about placing her. I couldn't help but have a feeling of freedom also.

I began visiting all the nursing homes in our area. I found one close to home that did not have a secure memory care unit, but the doctor rejected it. He said he was afraid Bridget would fight being placed and would therefore try to leave to go home. She hadn't wandered before, but I agreed she would be difficult. I found another skilled nursing home that had a secure memory care unit.

I didn't have a clue how to get her to the nursing home. I knew she would go screaming and fighting. I was outright scared for her and for me. I asked the doctor for his suggestions on how I could get her to go. He said he would be the bad guy and do it, if I could bring her to his office. I thought that might work, except it would ruin Bridget's relationship with him. He said that it was his job and it would work out in the long run.

Without Bridget knowing anything about the plan, I took her to the doctor. He sat across from her and softly told her he thought it best for her to spend a little time in a nursing home to get her weight up. She objected and he tried several times. The more he tried the more she objected. She stamped her feet up and down, pounded her fists on her thighs and screamed, "No! No! No!"

I felt like crying as I left the office to give them time alone. The doctor followed me into the hall after a few more futile minutes. He said the nursing home shuttle was unavailable and asked if I thought I could take her there. I said I'd try.

I told Bridget I would take her home. I had long before learned that sometimes I needed to tell a little fib. Perhaps a more socially correct phrase is a 'therapeutic lie'. I used it now to distract her, but felt it was another marker that our relationship, as we knew it, was over. Lying to her made me feel guilty and very sad. It is risky to tell such a lie because, if caught lying, trust is broken when it is needed most.

Fortunately, the nursing home was located between the doctor's office and home. We pulled into a parking spot in front and I had no idea what to do next. I got out of the car and went inside to tell admissions we were there and returned to the car. In a few minutes the director of memory care came out and engaged us in conversation. She invited us to go in for a visit. Bridget would not go in.

She asked if I would allow Bridget to have a sedative injection to calm her down. We waited 30 minutes for full effect and she reluctantly agreed to enter the building. We got as far as the reception lobby before Bridget would go no farther.

These people were compassionate professionals who knew what they were doing. They treated us with respect and were calm as they handled Bridget through the whole ordeal. They earned my trust right then. Nevertheless, I was an emotional wreck. We were drugging Bridget, against her will, so we could lock her up for the rest of her life in a memory care unit.

With no further progress, the director asked if I would help give Bridget another tranquilizer injection. More deception! I stood her up and gave her a hug and held her in my arms while the nurse injected her again. After another thirty minutes Bridget was limp as a noodle. The nurses stood her up and I led the way, so she would follow me. They each took an arm and we slowly walked down the hall and into the unit.

It was another huge blow when they suggested I not come to visit for a couple of weeks, to let Bridget adjust to her surroundings and new routines. I didn't want her to feel abandoned. Otherwise, she would identify with me and want to go home. I visited two days later anyway.

When I walked in, I saw an alarming sight. Bridget was sitting on a bench, dressed to go home, with her hands folded, like a ten-year-old waiting for a bus. Her belongs were all folded next to her. She was packed and ready to come home. When I approached, she stood up, grabbed both my wrists tightly, looked in my face and demanded, "Take me home!" I talked to her calmly with no thought of complying.

She repeated, "Take me home!" I tried to soothe her. As her emotions escalated I caught the eye of two CNAs who were talking and had not noticed us. I shuffled toward them with Bridget firmly attached to my wrists. I said, "We need help." They read the situation and distracted her so I could make my getaway. I got the message about giving new patients time to adjust. I did not return for two weeks. Even though my doctor wanted me to place her and I knew she was where she needed to be, I was still feeling guilty. I hated what I had done. The words I heard in my support group rang true, "I have been lovingly responsible.", but I still felt terrible. *Fred's story continues in Chapter 6.*

Brenda's story continues

After Tom's adventurous drive on the San Juan Scenic Byway he continued to slip deeper into his dementia. Brenda was caring for him full time and attending to every need. She was going it alone and not needing any outside resources. Then, it happened.

Tom was cooperative most of the time. He didn't speak often, and his words were garbled. I would ask him questions and he would wag his head yes or no. Sometimes I just had to guess what he was trying to say. I was frustrated because I couldn't communicate with him. He walked around the house all the time and I had to watch him carefully, because he would walk out the door. Tom's appetite was good. He was strong and was still the gentle man I had always known.

When the kids visited, they saw changes in Tom that I had missed. They kept after me to place him, but I was determined to take care of him at home. They pitched in when I needed them, so it wasn't as though I was the Lone Ranger. They became more concerned about me than their father and that bothered me. I was focused on him and not me.

The kids kept hounding me and I got upset with them. They started telling me I ought to go to a support group. I have never been a joiner, but I thought I'd go to one, just to get them off my back. I had a neighbor who facilitated a support group, so I ran out of excuses. The best thing I ever did for myself was to go and I soon became a regular attender.

I was doing well after I got some home-care assistance, with our children pitching in as well. They never gave up the pressure to place Tom into a nursing home. I reluctantly checked out several and found one only half a mile away from the house that I liked. I listened to others in the support group share their experiences of placing their loved ones. Every one of them had a common experience - that something happened to their loved one and the decision to place was made for them. When I'd ask the big question, the answer was, "It [the decision to place] will fall into your lap."

Tom had finished breakfast. I was at the counter putting dishes in the dishwasher and turned around just as he slumped over. I was able to break his fall to the floor. He was unconscious. I called 911 and the

EMTs quickly responded and took him to the hospital. He regained consciousness and was admitted. The doctor determined that Tom had had a seizure.

The doctor said that he should go directly to a nursing home. He was concerned about my inability to take care of Tom at home, because he would continue to fall, and I wouldn't be able to get him up. Tom was six foot two and weighed 230 pounds. I'm not physically strong enough to lift him. There was no question that Tom needed to have skilled nursing care. Tom was transported from the hospital directly to the nursing home. He was a little out of it but adapted rather quickly and better than I expected. He will never come home again and I'm okay with that. *Brenda's story continues in Chapter 5.*

Charlotte's story continues

It has been a long journey for Charlotte. She did all she could to take care of Carl whose Parkinson's disease had reduced him to a shell of who he had been. She was on the threshold of a nervous breakdown and he was nearing the end of his life. She had one more major decision to make.

I loved Carl and hated what Parkinson's was doing to him and to me. Toward the late stage of Parkinson's he couldn't follow a conversation and just stared into space while pretending to watch TV. During his last few days at home, he fell several times and I had to call 911 for help, since I couldn't get him up by myself. Once, when I was helping him into bed, he suddenly looked at me with fear in his eyes, grabbed my arm and pleaded, "Don't hurt me!" That about broke my heart, but I realized then that he needed to be placed in a care facility for our mutual safety. It was my "Moment of Decision." How could I take care of him when he was afraid of me and within a few minutes could possibly become a threat to me?

I had investigated different nursing home, while thinking that I could take care of him right up to the end. I was fortunate to find a good nursing home. I placed him without any resistance. Carl wasn't aware of his new surroundings and settled in quickly. I got into the swing of things, attending a care conference, and visited Carl frequently. He was unresponsive to my being there, but I went to see him regardless. Sometimes I think visiting him was more for my benefit than for his. He passed away in five months.

Looking back, I wish that I would have known more about Parkinson's and what caring for Carl would entail. I know that the symptoms and deficiencies vary. Each day brought new challenges that I had to find ways to handle, without the tools to give him the best care and at the same time take care of myself. *Charlotte's story continues in Chapter 6.*

Linda's story continues

Linda committed to be her mother's caregiver. She sacrificed her own well-being to give all her attention to her mother. Linda had no knowledge of dementia and had no idea how to cope and even less, how to take care of herself.

I was consumed with taking care of my mother. I gave up my personal time and didn't have any time to myself for a quite a while. I was sad and angry. We did have some good laughs and lighter times, but mostly I was just trying to stay on top of everything. I realized I needed to make time for myself and looked for ways to do that. I joined the gym.

I wish I would have known the prognosis of her condition before I took on the role as her caregiver. I had no idea what was ahead for me. If my brother and I had gotten together earlier and gotten a diagnosis we could have made better decisions regarding her future care. I don't think the average doctor or therapist has much insight to help caregivers cope with their new role. The doctors could have been more sympathetic and helpful.

When mother had her will updated, she insisted on leaving her entire estate to me, which I strenuously objected to. When my brother found out he turned against me. I assured him that when she died I would give him half the estate. He still wouldn't have anything to do with me. I think that he wasn't as mad at me as he was hurt. He had given so much of himself to mom's care and then for some unknown reason, she rejected him. He took out his hurt and anger on me. I was hurt but forgave him; I knew he was hurting, too.

After mom left my brother out of her will, the only support I had was from my daughters, a niece, and a couple very close friends. A bright spot appeared a few months later when a friend suggested I join a caregiver support group. I met other caregivers who were facing similar circumstances, and it was so helpful to hear how they handled their situations. It was in that group that I learned about resources that I needed. I was part of a group of caregivers who truly cared about each other. For some of us our group was an important social contact because it meant being with folks who understood each other.

As her memory worsened it was becoming apparent that mom was going to need full-time care. I was wearing out and I started the process to place her, but I had planned a short vacation and would take care of that when I got back. *Linda's story continues in Chapter 6.*

Roger's story continues

Betty Jo was going to day care, physical therapy, and participating in activities galore, but she was slipping away. She came to the point of not recognizing Roger as her husband and that bothered him at first, but he had survived so many of her hallucinations that he learned how to handle them. Then a dramatic life-changing event hit in the middle of the night.

It was three o'clock in the morning and I was sound asleep when I was suddenly being shaken. I woke up, opened my eyes and saw a very bright white light. A deep voice asked, "What's your name?" A shiny policeman's badge reflected in the beam of his flashlight. I answered and he told me to get up. I put on my robe and without a word, he walked me out to the living room.

Betty Jo stood there talking to another officer. She saw me and hysterically screamed, "Arrest that man. He's not my husband!" I stood there in disbelief, devastated. She was hysterical and the officer was trying to calm her down. The officer who stood next to me asked for identification. I explained that she had dementia and he believed me.

It took a while, but she began to calm down as the officer assured her that I was indeed her husband and asked if it would be okay if I slept in the guest bedroom. She agreed and all quieted down. I didn't sleep much the rest of the night or most nights thereafter.

The next morning she asked me why I slept in the guest bed. She had no memory of the night before. I reported this to our social worker at PACE. I felt like I was in a trap and no way out. If there was a light at the end of the tunnel, it was probably the train of despair coming. I was scared.

A week later at two o'clock in the morning the phone rang. The 911 operator said, "You need to talk to a policeman at your front door." The adrenaline hit me. Kids or grandkids ... something has happened! I got up, opened the door and asked what was going on.

The officer answered, "It's about your wife. She's five houses down the street." Betty Jo had walked out into the cold night. She was in her night gown, walking barefoot in the ice and snow. It was 15 degrees. She got cold and rang a neighbor's doorbell. The lady who answered the door was new to the neighborhood. Betty Jo didn't know her name or where she lived. The neighbor called 911. The officer who responded had been to our house and knew the situation. He brought Betty Jo home. I warmed her up and got her into bed.

The next morning Betty Jo had no memory of her outdoor adventure. I called our social worker and reported what had happened. I was afraid for Betty Jo. If she had fallen on the ice or if she had stayed in the cold much longer she could have died of hypothermia. I told her what she had done and although she couldn't remember, this time she didn't argue: this was not negotiable. I was ready to throw my hands up in surrender. We needed to do something. I couldn't take it much longer. But I was put on hold for another day. *Alan's story continues in Chapter 5.*

Bill's story (as told to Glen)

Bill was a World War II veteran and was an independent man. He and his wife had raised their children and had a good life together. He saw himself as a husband and not his wife's caregiver, but a time came when his wife needed more care than he could give. Nevertheless, he was doing the best that he could until control was taken away from him.

I am 93 years old and my wife Hazel is 92. We have been married 72 years. We raised four children who now live with their families scattered across the country. A few years ago, her memory was getting noticeably worse. We went to our doctor and he examined her and declared her incompetent to manage her own affairs. Our daughter and I had dual Powers of Attorney to manage her medical and financial affairs. I was doing the best that I could to take care of her.

I thought life was going well, but I did need help taking care of the house so I hired a housekeeper to come twice a week. Things were going smoothly. Then one day Hazel had a really rough day. Looking back now, I think she was having memory problems and she got confused easily. We didn't go to a doctor to have her checked for dementia.

Hazel went to bed early. One of our sons called and wanted to talk to her, but I told him that she had had a bad day and was asleep and I didn't want to waken her. He demanded that I wake her up and threatened to call the police if I refused. He must have thought that I was abusing her or something like that. So I woke her up and I don't know what they talked about. I didn't realize it at the time, but our kids were more concerned about their mother than I realized.

The kids accused me of being stubborn. We just didn't see things the same way and they didn't respect my opinion. My goal was to take care of her by myself and keep her at home for as long as possible. They didn't think I was up to the job. I felt like they didn't trust me and that hurt. They couldn't help me, because they all lived so far away.

The day after our son called, I went to a doctor's appointment. The housekeeper was cleaning and being there for Hazel. I found out later that as soon I left, Hazel told her that she was afraid of me and thought I was going to kill her, and she was becoming hysterical. The caregiver was trained to call the police when she thought someone was in danger. The responding officer listened to her and radioed for Adult Protective Services (APS) to come to the house.

When I came home there was a policeman and all these people in my house and I didn't know who they were or what was going on. I was confused and got really angry. Then the man from APS asked Hazel if she wanted to stay home with me or go to a nursing home. She said she wanted to go.

I was heartbroken. I couldn't believe what she just said. Nobody asked me my opinion and I was ignored, totally helpless, and I couldn′t do anything for her. The officer and APS took her out the door and wouldn't even let me get close to her. I felt like she was being kidnapped right in front of me and there was nothing I could do. Everybody left and I was alone and mad as a hornet.

I was beside myself with grief and anger. Even after they put her into a nursing home, they wouldn't let me go near her and I didn't know what was happening to her. I wanted to be with her and to take care of her or at least see to it that she was well taken care of.

I was alone at home trying to understand what was happening. I began to blame myself for being a failure as a husband. I tortured myself remembering so many of the times in our marriage when I had been selfish and I thought then how I must have hurt her so many times over the years. Yet, I loved her and I was a provider and protector for my family– just as my father had modeled for me. That is what men of my generation did. Apparently, that wasn't good enough for her or our children. I guess that's why I feel like such a failure.

The facility where Hazel was placed was associated with PACE. A social worker contacted me and gave me a book written by a local author who was a volunteer peer-coach who helped caregivers. She gave me his phone number and told me to call and I did.

That first day we met I had a real pity party. I poured out my feelings of anger, guilt, pain, and the horrible feeling of being betrayed by my own children who turned against me. I felt like the rug had been pulled out from under me and I couldn't get up, and the ones I thought should help me … didn't. He quietly listened and didn't give me any advice or judge me.

I had many sessions with him. He shared from his own experiences how his wife had become desperately afraid of him to the point that he couldn't take care of her at home. Listening to someone who had experienced what I was going through gave me hope.

I was so alone. When Christmas came, I had no one to be with. They wouldn't let me even see Hazel on Christmas Day. My coach was also alone, so we shared our Christmas dinner together. That was the loneliest Christmas in my life. My wife was alive and they wouldn't let me see her. I can't go on this way. *Bill's story continues in Chapter 5.*

Donna's story continues

Donna had been going it alone for so long that her health was beginning to go downhill. She wasn't sleeping or eating right, and she was wearing out. She had given up her social life and was becoming a homebound, desperate recluse. She had no support team to help her. She admitted to being just a "tiny bit" stubborn, but pain, whether it be physical or mental, shocks us into reality and she did act.

Howard's incontinence worsened. I couldn't take him out, because he would have an embarrassing accident. He would defecate wherever he was. Then he got to smearing feces on himself and on the walls of the bathroom. It seemed that all I was doing was following him around, mopping, deodorizing and shampooing the carpet. I was getting more and more depressed trying to keep up. I love him so much, but I was losing sleep, not eating or taking care of myself. I heard about compassion fatigue, which comes as a result of long-term exposure to pain and stress. My compassion fatigue was off the chart.

I sought help from the Area Agency on Aging (AAA) and found them helpful by guiding me toward some adult daycare. Howard enjoyed the activities and social interaction. I began to get a little time for myself and I started going to a caregiver support group where I found the emotional support I needed. They shared experiences that gave me ideas how to deal with some of the same problems. I used what worked for me. We shared our stories, laughed and cried together. Some of us were closer to each other than our own families. It was fun to share and to encourage one another to hang in there when the going was tough.

I knew that someday I would not be able to keep up the pace of being Howard's caregiver at home and would have to place him into a care center. The financial burden would be overwhelming, but I was near the end of my rope. I went to an attorney to get help with financial planning. He told me that we were too late to save all the assets we had worked so hard to accumulate for our retirement years. I could see that most of our assets would be going toward his long-term care in a nursing home. It was a fearful thing to worry about, that if I ever needed long term care, there would be no money left. I'll leave that up to the Lord.

Howard had diabetes and I had been giving him his insulin shots for years, but one day as I was injecting the insulin, he hit me with his fist. That made me mad and I hit him back. I was astonished at my own reaction and I thought, "O my God, this could be construed as elder abuse." I knew that wasn't good at all, but I had really wanted to hit him. He had made me so mad.

That was a game changer for me. His incontinence, and his not allowing me to take care of him, was more than I could bear. That was my "Moment of Decision" to place him into a nursing home. I just couldn't take it anymore. The physical and emotional stress had become overwhelming. I'm glad that I had checked out the nursing homes in our area before I decided to place him. *Donna's story continues in Chapter 5.*

Faye's Story continues

When Jake was in the early stages of dementia he was an 'easy keeper'. He was cooperative, in relatively good physical health, and Faye was able to say with confidence, "I can handle this," but Faye's caregiver burden was becoming unbearable and she was ready to collapse into the pit of compassion fatigue. Guilt plagued her when she admitted to herself that she needed professional help, but where she lived there wasn't any.

Late one evening as I was getting Jake ready for bed, he became agitated and suddenly fell to the floor. He was not moving. I immediately called 911 and our local EMTs responded and quickly rushed him 45 miles to the nearest hospital. Tests revealed that he had had a seizure.

The doctor made the decision and gave orders for him to be placed into a nursing home. They transported him directly from the hospital to the only nursing home in that town. My coach had told me that the decision to place Jake might just fall into my lap. That is exactly what happened. The doctor made the decision and I just followed orders.

When I got home later that night, I turned on the lights. I have never experienced such quiet or felt so alone. I cried and sobbed until I was exhausted. I guess I had so much emotion stored up inside of me that the dam broke and my tears released my pent-up feelings. I was relieved that Jake was where he needed to be. He was safe and would be taken care of (so I thought).

I drove the 45 miles to see him almost daily at first. When winter snows made driving our narrow mountain highway too dangerous, I didn't go as often. That didn't seem to bother him as he had lost track of time. He recognized me as someone who cared for him and he was always glad to see me. One day I told him that we were married and that I was his wife of 35 years. He quickly responded, gesticulating and guffawing, "Oh no, no, no, no," as if he would never have chosen me. We both laughed and hugged, an unexpected light moment that I will always cherish among the sorrow.

I kept busy catching up with a lot of chores that I'd had to put aside. I started playing bridge again and visited Jake several times a week. It seemed like a chapter of my life had closed and a new one was opening, but not the way I anticipated. *Faye's story continues in Chapter 5.*

Juanita's story

This story was contributed by Juanita's family who wanted her story shared so that caregivers might consider planning end-of-life issues sooner than later.

Juanita and Virgil retired and moved to Western Colorado. They loved the mountains and rural lifestyle. Juanita was the hiker who led many hiking groups to isolated panoramas to see wildflowers, wildlife, pristine waters, and to experience the solitude of the high country.

They enjoyed their country home for several years before health issues came upon Virgil. He was diagnosed with hydrocephalus that caused him to lose his balance and fall, and his gait became a shuffle. This disease can also cause dementia and he was having trouble remembering things. He was still able to do many of the things he enjoyed and was safe in and around the house.

For many years they had enjoyed traveling in their RV around the country. Even with Virgil's condition they continued to travel far and wide with Juanita doing all the driving. Before long, however, he had to use a walker and became more house bound. Other complications also degraded his lifestyle.

Virgil never lost his cognitive ability, but he became totally dependent on Juanita. She didn't think of herself as a caregiver until after she went to a caregiver conference. She joined the ranks of caregivers and began going to a support group. Having been a college professor she was a great student and came to the group to learn all she could from those who shared how they coped with their loved one´s condition. She picked up those ideas that worked for her. She also knew she had to take care of herself. For her, that meant continuing to enjoy her outdoor pursuits, photography, and hiking the high country.

When asked about needing help, she responded, "I can handle it." During the group discussion someone asked, "What happens to Virgil if you die first?" to which she responded that, because of his incurable disease, he would most likely die first and she was "healthy as a horse."

Juanita's daughter shares *"The Rest of the Story"*

> Mom and dad drove from Colorado up here to Montana to be with our family. I think mom was suspicious that she had leukemia, but she did not

tell anyone. The doctor had told her that something was wrong, but she wanted to join us on our family trip to Oregon so bad. He told her it would be fine to travel and that they could look into it when she returned. She figured because of dad's bad health this would be the last time all of us would have the opportunity to go on a vacation together. She had a stent put in her heart about two weeks before they left for our trip.

I don't know what caused her to get so sick on our trip. We found that she had about two liters of fluid around her lungs when she ended up in the emergency room in a tiny coastal Oregon town. In the process of trying to find out what was wrong, they discovered the problem with her white blood cells, leading them to check further.

It was a bizarre journey trying to decide where she could receive the best care. We spent a week in Corvallis before the doctors told us she needed to go to a larger medical facility. They wanted her to go to Portland, but that wasn't possible as we have no family there. We decided to bring her here to Kalispell, as we have an amazing oncology department. We drove through the night to get here. It was the week of the solar eclipse and there were no places to stay anywhere in Oregon, and we needed to get her home.

Unfortunately, we previously had no conversations about dad's care in case something had happened to her. You know, she was the healthy one! She had said that she was reaching a point where she couldn't take care of him. I don't know how much she had discussed this with dad. Unfortunately, the only place in our house for anyone to stay is upstairs or in the basement. We had no safe place for dad to stay. Within a few days we found a wonderful memory care place here where he could stay while we were getting mom settled in the hospital here.

While mom was in the hospital some ladies from her church flew from Colorado to visit her for a couple days. How precious it was to mom to connect with friends. It meant so much to our family to experience the depth of her influence and how much her friends loved her—enough that they went to the expense and effort to attend to her in her last days.

The whole thing was insane, you could never come up with the scenario. Mom and dad never went back to their home in Colorado. When my brother went to their house to begin to pack their stuff after mom passed away, there was folded laundry in the laundry room, waiting to be put away. I suppose my point in telling you all of that is to emphasize how important it is to have discussions with your family, even if one family member seems to be the picture of health. Mom could out-hike, out-kayak, and out-ski me until that last summer. And, travel with your medical files. She always had dad's when they traveled but not her own.

We talked things over with dad. He didn't want to spend the winter in Montana, so my brother took him all the way to Texas. Dad lived near my brother in a memory care unit in a fine nursing home where until he died a few months later.

The Forest View

Your self-image becomes wrapped up into one word: CAREGIVER. It seems to define all you are. As time goes on, you begin to burn out, which spawns physical ailments, depression and even a nervous breakdown. Unfortunately, too many of us resist getting help. Notice how many stories report that caregivers reached out for help only when they hit bottom. Think about getting help before that. As it turns out, if caregivers don't get help early, they burn out faster and place their loved ones sooner.

When a loved one first shows suspicious symptoms that may be the time to discuss the future. If possible, this is a good time for a family discussion. A word of caution to adult children: Listen to your parents and their desires. Avoid imposing your perceptions and solutions on them. You want them to be safe, but they want to be independent. What may be a solution in your mind may be an obstacle for a parent. Forcing our will on someone else breeds resentment and mistrust at a time when love and trust are so important.

Don't keep you loved one at home just because they made you promise to never put them in a nursing home. Keeping such a promise can be a big mistake. You must do what's best for them and for you. Your love one could seriously injure themselves or leave the stove burners on. You could burnout and fail to care well. You could ruin your health. When your loved one said, "Don't place me.", they were not thinking of an expensive, long-term disease. Nor were you. When a grave situation changes everything, your decisions are different. Imagine having a conversation about placement when your loved one was much younger. Ask yourself what they would have wanted if they could have seen themselves now. Often, they would have asked to be placed, to relieve you.

All of us need to consider end-of-life decisions. Write down your wishes and advance medical directives. Who should make decisions if you are incapacitated? Communicate your desires to the entire family. End of life planning is mostly for the family. It reduces worry and disagreements.

When you visit someone in a nursing home, you are a visitor. You walk down the hallways and see residents asleep in wheelchairs with their mouths open. You hear someone calling for help. It's not as good as home. It's natural to react to the décor and crowding.

When you go to check out a facility with the intent of placing your loved one, you need a different mindset. Don't think about your feelings; think about what is best for your loved one. It's not about, "How can I do this to the one I love?" It's about, "Where will my loved one be best cared for." Your goal is to place them where they will be comfortable and get the care they need. You are not moving in, your loved one is.

Some places have lovely reception areas. They are appealing when you first walk in. If your loved one will be in memory care, they may always be behind a locked door. How does it look back there? You are usually thinking about how your loved one feels right now and how they will react to the new environment. Most loved ones are unhappy at first but adapt to the environment. They will be in the hands of professional caregivers who know how to compassionately manage their residents. And as your loved one declines, they will not care much about décor.

Quality of care is what matters. Check with the state for complaint and inspection reports. Talk to anyone you know who has placed someone. Talk to the head of care and the head nurse. Are you looking for assisted living, skilled nursing care, or a memory care? Find out all you can ahead of time, because there are often waiting lists. Is the price all-inclusive or a base rate with added charges for new needs?

When you begin checking out care facilities, your initial contact will most likely be a marketing representative. He or she will give you a tour the physical plant, but you won't have much interaction with the staff. A good way to find out how staff treats residents is to visit without an appointment, even after hours. Does anyone greet you? Are they happy in their work? Do they listen to residents or herd them around? Visit more than once.

Don't forget the drive time and convenience of the location. If it's too far away, you may not visit as often. In the beginning, you will be making lots of trips. Over time, wear and tear on you and your vehicle mount up.

In any event, the time may come when every reasonable effort at home care has been made and home care is no longer an option. You may decide on, or circumstances will require, placement. The feelings we have after placement are conflicting. On one hand, you are sad and feel guilty. On the other hand, you know you did the right thing and are relieved. You may on occasion second-guess the decision, but time will prove you were right.

When you get home the first time, home may seem very quiet. You may feel totally alone. You have lost your job. You are not the primary caregiver anymore. You feel adrift.

On the other hand, you may sleep well for the first time in years. You can choose what to do. You may also feel guilty for enjoying anything. Friends may be glad to see you. Some may think you are completely free, and others may not want you to have too much fun.

Your job as a home caregiver may be finished, but you will become an advocate on a team of skilled professional caregivers. Your loved one will continue to need your love and your oversight of the professional caregivers. After the decision to place, you can say to yourself, "I have been lovingly responsible."

In 2020 the world was turned upside down by the coronavirus covid-19. The elderly and those with health conditions are highly susceptible to contagion and deadly virus. Nursing homes are secured so that caregivers cannot visit. Those residents who were near death even before the virus hit, were not allowed to have visitors. The emotional impact is devastating.

Home caregivers (along with everyone else) began living with government-imposed guidelines. We began hearing the phrase "Social Distancing" and seeing people wear face masks. Most stores were closed and those deemed essential ran out of toilet paper, disinfectants and some food items. When "Stay at Home" restrictions were announced, caregivers lost what support they had from family and friends. There was a fear that people could bring the virus into the house and infect the caregiver and loved one alike. The caregiver was even more isolated.

Those being cared for had difficulty understanding what was going on. Loved ones were disturbed by the changing social structure and changing routines. Demented patients could not grasp the reasons for those changes and their anxiety made it more difficult for them to be managed.

Nursing homes adapted by restricting access and taking extra precautionary measures to protect their staffs as well as the vulnerable residents. Caregivers were able in some cases to use a computer to have contact. Residents could sit in front of a window and talk on the phone to a caregiver standing outside the facility.

Because numerous nursing homes across the country experienced high infection and mortality rates, family caregivers may be more reluctant to place a loved one in a facility. It is difficult enough to place someone, but with the fear of putting them in a high-risk environment causes caregivers to recoil.

In all these stories you read how resilient caregivers overcome adversity. Regardless of how covid-19 develops, caregivers will find ways to take care of their loved ones and themselves.

Chapter 5

Advocate: I advise and protect

If you place your loved one in a care facility, your caregiving role changes dramatically. You no longer provide hands-on care; instead you become your loved one's advocate on a team of professional caregivers. You are now the voice of your loved one, an intermediary, and a protector. The secret to be an effective advocate is to be an active member of the team.

Institutional living takes a lot of adjustment for both of you. It can be daunting to change from doing everything to be an observer. Staff has to learn what you both need and expect. Heavily regulated facilities have structure, schedules, and procedures that take a while to learn. For instance, how to access the building after hours, getting around in the building, and meeting key staff members. You will soon learn who has the answers to your questions. All this requires time and patience.

It might be useful to find a chair and just observe residents and staff. How comfortable is your loved one when he or she doesn't know you are watching? Which staff members have the answers? Who is especially caring and attentive? Each staff member has a different personality and level of experience. Some are eager to help and are compassionate. A few are going through the motions and some are only working for a paycheck.

It takes time for the staff to get acquainted with your loved one and you. It's up to you to introduce them to what your loved one likes and dislikes. They in turn will ask you questions and share their observations. Communicate!

You may be especially sensitive to things that don't go right. You may second guess yourself and be impatient with how they treat your loved one. However, it doesn't serve you well to start off with criticisms and demands.

Hang back and watch before you jump in. Most concerns can be settled in care conferences and conversations. Be a positive helpful member of your loved one's care team. Take notes of your visits and names so you will know who does what. Keep your support team and family informed, not only about the status of your loved one but also how you are coping. Staff will be more likely to give you support and be there when you need them.

Advocate: I advise and protect

Ted-I was relieved
Dwight-I was okay
Fred-I got involved
Donna-I had to pay extra
Rosa-Skilled care all the way
Bill-She wasn't scared of me anymore
Connie-When care went haywire
Brenda-It was more like kindergarten
Roger-I was part of the care team
Faye-They kept kicking him out
The Forest View

Ted's story continues

Ted was a good caregiver and was taking care of himself. He understood his wife's disease and prognosis. He had come to terms with the fact that she would never get better and he had done all he could to make her comfortable. Gaining the support of his estranged family added to his being able to manage Flo's care. He learned to cope with her behaviors that he attributed to her dementia. The decision to place her into a nursing home was upon him.

Flo had fallen several times, but one day she fell and I couldn't get her up. While I held her hand and tried to comfort her until the ambulance arrived, it came to me that this was my 'Moment of Decision' falling into my lap. I'd heard that phrase in my support group and that is what happened to me. As much as I loved her, I knew down deep in my heart that there was no way I could continue to care for her at home. I knew I wasn't a failure and I didn't feel guilty, but I was very sad.

Because I had planned I was able to quickly place her into a nursing home. By this time Flo was unaware of being placed and it was actually a more peaceful transition than I ever expected. Flo's doctor, the PACE team, and the nursing home medical staff continued to take care of her.

I started my new role as her advocate. I filled out a questionnaire about Flo's background, her likes, dislikes, fears; things that made her happy and interesting talking points. I went to the state mandated care conferences where I wrote down questions and shared my observations. I was asked for suggestions to address issues that I thought were important. We developed a high level of trust that resulted in better care for Flo and reduced my stress.

My experience was most positive and I am satisfied and pleased with the care she received. I really appreciated our social worker who checked in on me periodically to see how I was surviving. I visited Flo frequently, we ate meals together, and I took her for drives to get her outside until she was no longer responsive and her incontinence increased.

Flo lived in the nursing home only eight months before she passed on. I will always grieve losing her, but I have moved forward, without regret. *Teds story continues in Chapter 6.*

Dwight's story continues:

Dwight was a loving son who put his career on hold to care for his mother. No matter how much he loved her, there came the time when the caregiver burden was so heavy that he couldn't carry it anymore. His mother's blindness, anxiety, and other complications were overwhelming both of them. Dwight was down to his last option.

It took five days to get mom calmed down from her worst anxiety attack. She checked herself into the hospital briefly and from there went to a rehabilitation facility for six weeks. I was there every day. I was temporarily relieved of having the responsibility of caring for her and I had some time to recuperate. I couldn't help sleeping with 'one ear open' all night and woke from a deep sleep thinking that she was calling my name. I was an emotional wreck and ready to explode over the slightest hassle. My caregivers' group was my lifeline and helped me stay sane.

When mom came home from the nursing home I made some changes. I hired a home care assistance company to help mom with such things as dressing, bathing and being there for her. When they were there I went for a walk around the block or ran an errand. That time away was good for my outlook.

I knew this arrangement wouldn't last. I was haunted by the thought of how I was going to be able to make the decision that mom needed long-term care. I listened to other caregivers in my support group who shared how that their decisions to place their loved one into a facility were made. In each case something happened that was out of their control, which took away all options except for long-term care in a nursing home. I wondered if something like that was going to happen to me.

Then it happened. Mom was having an anxiety attack that had gone on for more than 20 hours, I could not get her to the bathroom or even get her out of her chair. She was flailing her arms. At that moment I accepted that I was physically unable to care for her any longer. No matter how much I love her; no matter how much I want to help; no matter what I do, it isn't enough. I had to let someone else with the skills, resources, and facilities do this job I had been doing for the past eight years. At first I felt like a failure but having listened to other caregivers who had gone through similar circumstances, I knew I wasn't a failure. They validated my feelings and I knew down deep I couldn't have done anymore.

Mom had already spent time in the nursing home and much of the paperwork was already in place. I didn't have any complications. I placed her and she has adapted quite well. I am still her caregiver but in a new role as her advocate. I attend all the care conferences and I am kept informed on a regular basis, and if there is change in her condition, or if the doctor suggests a change in medication.

I am at peace that I made the right decision to place mom. She is where she needs to be with professional caregivers. I have found them to be compassionate and caring and very good at managing her. I am a member of mom's care team. I have a new role now and I'm finding it far less stressful. I'm more at ease knowing they really take good care of her. I found a new job and I'm getting my life back.

Fred's story continues:

Fred had taken care of Bridget at home for seven years. He thought he could continue taking care of her far longer, but his doctor said that it was time to place her. Fred experienced a horrific ordeal the day he placed Bridget into a nursing home. He knew he had done the right thing and she was where she needed to be to receive the best possible care. He had more adjusting to do.

I came home after our placement ordeal and stood in the middle of our living room feeling emotionally drained. I had just survived the most stressful time of my life. I took a deep breath and slowly exhaled with a sigh of relief. I noticed the quiet like I had never experienced it before. The house was still and profoundly different. I felt very alone. A tectonic shift in our relationship and my life had just occurred. It wasn't frightening, just eerie.

While I was absorbed in the quiet, my eyes fell on an artificial flower arrangement on the fireplace mantel. It was aged and lifeless. The thought came that I had never liked it. Without a moment's hesitation, I picked it up, took it to the garage and put it in the trash. It felt good. I tried it again with other things I didn't like, all impersonal knickknacks that meant nothing to me.

I was taking possession of my space; the beginning of a process that continues. I was not being disrespectful or rejecting Bridget. I didn't discard any personal items like clothes or pictures. She was still a strong presence in the house. I was just shifting my thinking from sharing decisions with her to making them on my own. This was a subconscious act that signified the beginning the rest of my life and that Bridget was a shrinking part of my life.

I began focusing on myself, because I was no longer providing her care, with that part of the job having been delegated. Even though our doctor had encouraged Bridget's placement, I still felt some guilt that I had failed. It made me want to be sure staff was doing it right.

In the beginning she begged me to take her home. I decided to just not respond. It seemed hardhearted, but there could be no negotiating. Over time she stopped asking, and later she told someone, "This is my home now."

At first, I looked for ways to please her. I took her the flavored bottled water she liked, brought her a smoothie, and brought things from home. It was nice to have her within two miles because it made travel easy for me. I befriended the staff and told them about Bridget's background, likes, and dislikes. The staff liked the family pictures I took, because they could talk about her life by having her share a memory, until her long-term memory also failed.

I occasionally joined her for meals and that let me get to know other residents. I found that interacting with staff and residents made it easier to feel part of the team. Sometimes I sat in a corner and watched how Bridget interacted with other residents. I complimented several staff for their obvious compassion and caregiving skills. There were times when Bridget just wouldn't cooperate and I was the only one to get her to comply. Staff saw me as a help, not a hindrance. My participating as her advocate led to improved care. I even got the direct phone number so could call direct to the unit, bypassing the switchboard that often delayed and sometimes failed to deliver messages.

Care conferences were a new and unpleasant experience at first. I thought the department heads were just complying with a state mandated waste of time. Each read their reports before I was asked what I might want to discuss. It seemed as if staff tried to impress me with the great job they were doing.

I wanted more input during the meetings. I wrote a letter to the director in which I asked for the staff to have name badges visible—not dangling from a belt. I had served on management teams professionally and we used first names and got to know each other. I also asked to speak first and raised questions about what was on my mind. Communicating about Bridget's condition and treatment were more important to me than a spreadsheet showing what percentage of meals she was eating. It helped greatly for me to take control of the process.

As time went on, I visited less frequently. There was less for me to do. Bridget became less responsive and with a shorter attention span. She was sleeping 16 to 18 hours a day near the end, so it was harder to drop in when she was awake. I've learned to be happy when I can connect with her, and less dejected when I can't. I still want to make her happy. *Fred's story continues in Chapter 6.*

Donna's story continues:

Donna found an adult day care facility for her husband. The hours he was there gave her some respite to begin taking care of herself. Eventually even the few hours of respite were not enough. She was burning out and decided it was time to find a nursing home:

I checked into several care centers and found one recommended by a friend. It seemed like a good fit. Our doctor coordinated all the arrangements and wrote the orders to place Howard. Placing him went smoothly. I was confident that he would settle in and receive the level of care he needed. When I took him to his new home, I told the administrator about his smearing feces on the walls at home and unshaken she responded, "Oh that happens. We call them 'Poocassos'. Her response broke the tension and I even laughed.

Howard settled in without fanfare and seemed content. It took a few weeks for me to get used to not taking care of his hourly needs. I visited him every day. I didn't know what to do with all the time I had on my hands. I realized how much of me had been taking care of him when he was at home.

I found out the hard way that care centers have different ways of providing service. The one I chose had an à la carte system. There was a base fee for room and board and then extra charges for many of the other needed services and supplies. I thought the base charge was very reasonable, but when I got the second bill I was astonished. I was charged for the extra care that CNAs gave for Howard's incontinence and even his diapers as well as other incidentals. I learned that with assisted living, there was no registered nurse to oversee medical services on site. No matter how minor a medical need might be, a resident was sent by ambulance to the hospital emergency room, whether it was an emergency or not and I had to pay.

I went in daily to visit and ended up changing diapers, cleaning him up, and I even helped in the kitchen. The facility was so understaffed and I found myself doing things I thought I was paying them to do. I was upset, so I met with the administrator and got nowhere, except for finding out why my bills were so high. I wasn't happy with the situation at all.

I talked to Howard's doctor about whether anything could be done regarding to control his incontinence. Finally, he prescribed a medicine that calmed his bowels. The amount of money I was spending each month went down as a result.

I don't go in to visit quite as often now. The activities director has involved Howard and he joins right in. He gets along well with the other residents and I'm more relaxed now.

Taking time for myself is a higher priority now that I have more time for myself and I'm slowly beginning to socialize. I am getting my life back, but occasionally I still feel guilty that I'm enjoying things that he can't experience anymore. I am not his on-sight caregiver, but I watch out for him. I try to work with the nursing staff.

I know that I made the right decision and he is where he needs to be. He is safe, well fed, and cared for, beyond what I could do for him at home. I'm renewing friendships, playing cards, going to the theater, enjoying the fellowship in my church family and I feel alive again. I'm still a loving caregiver.

Rosa's story continues

Rosa's brother was supposed to be looking after their parents, but instead he exploited them. She interceded and made the commitment to become their caregiver. As a long-distance caregiver she did what she could for her mom and dad, but she couldn't give them the care they needed.

The world seemed to be falling in on mom and dad. My brother was exploiting them financially. The senior community where they lived gave them a 90-day notice to move, because the facility could not provide the safety and level of care they now needed as a result of their declining health. Mother was taking opioids and kept passing out. Dad could not manage her oxygen and she was admitted to the hospital Intensive Care Unit (ICU) on two occasions.

It was up to me to become their caregiver. I resigned my job and found a new one four hours away. The more I was with them the more I realized they were in danger. I looked into an assisted living facility near my home where I could keep a close eye on them.

My brother was livid. He made vile accusations and spread untruths about my motives. He was fearful of losing access to their money. I didn't need his vitriol on top of the stress I had caring for our parents. This created a chasm between us that has lasted to this day.

On the other hand, my parent's family and friends were relieved that I had acted. Both reactions brought forth a great deal of pain. One was the cruelty of my brother turning against me which left me grieving the loss of our loving bond. Secondly, those who supported my decision also criticized me, because they thought I had waited too long to rescue them. It was like getting a pat on the back and a kick in the butt at the same time.

I arranged mom and dad's move into an assisted living center. Once they had settled in I visited them every day, managed their finances, arranged for new physician, brought them to my home for family dinners, managed the disbursement of their properties, provided phone and television service, and procured whatever else they needed.

Mother had always abused dad, so I told the staff to be on the alert for mother's abusiveness. When dad got a little difficult to handle at night, I had the nurse call and I went to calm him down. He always responded to me, but I lost a lot of sleep.

My boat was overloaded by working full time and tending to them. Though it was a labor of love, caregiving required the biggest share of my non-working time. I lost the joy of being my father's daughter. I became his parent. After three years in assisted living my father's condition worsened to the point of requiring full time care and was admitted to a memory care unit. At that time they could no longer afford assisted living and my mother was placed into long-term care as well.

I was happy for my parents being in a safe place. After dad's second day in memory care he took me down one of the hallways to show me a small chapel. He said, "I go in there every day to thank God that you brought me to this place." My father died within seven months. I had so much to be thankful for and I expressed my gratitude to my family, children, aunts, uncles and friends of my parents, the staff, personal friends, and strangers who lifted my spirits and supported me all the way.

Rosa's story didn't end with the passing of her father. She had more years ahead of her to care for her mother, which was a much different experience than caring for her father.

Mom had always been physically healthy and rarely visited a doctor. I talked her into seeing a new young doctor whom she came to like (like her grandson) and he was so good at talking her into a mental exam. He established rapport and even though she couldn't remember his name, she liked seeing him. He diagnosed her as having Mild Cognitive Impairment (MCI). He explained that she was having early symptoms of dementia. He didn't tell us anything about what we as caregivers were facing. He was so young that he couldn't have had much experience with caregiving, therefore had no practical advice to give us. I wish now that he would have suggested we start finding help and learning about caregiving.

I have been humbled knowing that millions of people walk this journey every day and night; knowing others' journeys are much more challenging than mine; knowing there are people out there who stand ready to take care of caregivers.

I have found joy in helping others. I know what it's like to take this complicated journey. I was enriched by finding resources and receiving training to understand how to work with dementia behaviors and families who must cope with them.

Looking back now, I would do a few things differently. I would not have ignored my dad's early symptoms and irrational behaviors. I would have put together a support team for me a lot sooner and I'd have started searching for resources long before I'd needed them. I am glad that I was determined to pass on to others the good that came from my caregiver journey. *Rosa's story continues in Chapter 6.*

Bill's story continues

Bill felt like the rug had been pulled out from under him after APS removed his wife from their home and into a nursing home without his consent. Her dementia had taken over and she had become afraid of him. Bill was doing all he could to take care of her at home and had hired help. He was doing the best he could, but it wasn't enough. He was now very alone but determined to restore what he could of his relationships.

I started going to a support group and I listened and learned more about caregiving. I wasn't looking for sympathy but answers to questions about caregiving. It was a couple of weeks before whoever oversaw Hazel's care agreed to let me see her while being accompanied by a staff person. Hazel didn't understand what was going on and it was several weeks before she lost all fear of my being there with her. Before long she welcomed me into her room. I brought her things she liked and she loved to see me. We ate many meals together.

Then one day she asked me to take her home. I really wanted to but I had concluded that I couldn't take care of her any longer and that she was in the right place. I knew she was safe, being attended to, and she began to feel that was her new home. I talked to the staff at care conferences and soon accepted that I was not her 'hands on' caregiver anymore. However, my loneliness increased like I had never experienced in my life. I've outlived most of my friends.

I was so angry with our kids! Each one was reaching out to me but rather than welcoming their overtures of reconciliation I, out of pride or some other part of me, rejected them. Then I would feel remorseful and even more alone. I found myself holding on grudges of the past. When they had come from across the country to be with their mother and me something would always come up and I would lash out at them and say something horrible that would drive them away. Then I hated myself for what I said.

My coach and I have shared many a lunch and hours of talking not only about issues of the past but also understanding the present. I have a friend who can talk hunting, fishing, with whom I can share memories of the outdoors. I am still wanting my family back more than anything else, but I can't seem to find a way to handle my feelings. It has been a couple of years now and I have been changed by all that has happened. I've mellowed out a lot and have come to accept that all in all things have worked out for the best for Hazel and me. I don't think about the past. Now I cherish the phone calls and visits of our kids. My animosity has left me. I've learned to be thankful for how our kids grew into fine people that I'm very proud of. I have a wife who I enjoy sharing a meal with, talking to and being together and I know she is where she needs to be. I am where I am and living life again.

After I interviewed and wrote Bill's story, he fell and broke his hip. His condition worsened. His children gathered around him as he laid unresponsive. They showered him with their love, reassured him that Hazel would be cared for. I held Bill's hand and when I told him I was there, he responded by squeezing my hand. A daughter read a Scripture from the Bible and a cell phone played comforting old hymns of faith. Because he was such an outdoorsman songs of the Sons of the Pioneers western music played in the background. Perhaps the lyrics didn't mean as much as those old familiar tunes that soothed his spirit.

What a blessing it was to witness loving compassion as a result of reconciliation that healed broken relationships and brought Bill's family together before his death.

Connie's story continues:

Sometimes a caregiver just has to take charge. Connie and her brother were not on the same page and it risked their relationship. She made a most difficult decisions when she placed their mother into a nursing home. Connie's caregiving burden and stress soon became replaced by the frustration of being their mother's advocate.

By having Medical Power of Attorney and control of mom's finances, I unilaterally placed mom into a memory care facility near me that I had researched with the help of my daughter. This, I'm sure, broke my brother's heart and he vented anger toward me and quit speaking to me at this point. I was stressed about placing mom and at the same time I loved my brother and seeing our relationship suffer was heart rending.

The only support I had now was from my daughters from a distance, a niece, and a couple very good and supportive friends. A bright spot that appeared a few months later was when a friend suggested I join a class for caregiver's support. The class met 4 or 5 times, and afterwards I continued with an informal group that met regularly at one of the churches. I met many others who were facing similar situations, and it was helpful to hear how they handled the situation, and about resources to provide help. We all supported each other. I'm still friends with several people from the groups.

At first I was relieved thinking that mom was safe and properly taken care of. I soon became aware that the care she was receiving was not adequate. Of course, she was extremely unhappy and wanted to leave all the time. By then, she was remembering her childhood and wanted to live with people from times past who had been dead for 50 years or more. I just went along with it and said we could check into it. I took her for frequent drives. My brother visited, too.

I became increasingly concerned about her safety and the lack of care I noticed at this facility. I visited daily and assumed a level of care that they weren't providing. I complained and met with the director with no meaningful results. I had to hire a lady to go into the facility to visit on the days that I could not be with mom. Conditions deteriorated to such a point that I contacted an ombudsman to intercede on my behalf. Eventually, I had mom transferred to a different care center where the care was much better, but at this point, she was already severely demented. She was accepted into hospice care and died two months later. During this time, my brother and I resolved our differences and now have a strong bond again.

We miss her but appreciate all the memories, recipes, flower seeds, and all the pictures, too. We believe we kept her comfortable in her own home as long as we could and, with all the love we had, did the best we could to caring for her in her final months. It sure wasn't easy, and I have a few regrets, but we both did the best we could in dealing with a disease that we had no knowledge about beforehand. We hadn't known how mercilessly it would turn all our lives upside down. I still feel a lot of guilt, but time is resolving that.

Brenda's story continues:

Brenda cared for Tom at home for several years. He was not a burden in the early stages of dementia, but as his condition deteriorated her workload increased dramatically. She only reluctantly sought help but was still reluctant about going to a support group. A few days after his harrowing drive over the San Juan Mountains, Tom had a seizure which led to Brenda's 'Moment of Decision' to place Tom into a skilled nursing facility.

After Tom recovered from his seizure our children and I went with Tom to the nursing home and left him there. A week later I started going to see him about every day. He seemed content in his new home. He wandered around and got along well with the other residents. When I went in to see him, he always smiled. He hadn't been talking for some time, but when I asked him questions he would shake his head yes or no. He could process some information but just couldn't express himself and that left both of us frustrated and sad.

I took his electric shaver with me and shaved him, combed his hair, and fussed over him. He liked the attention. He didn't like to take a shower though and it was a real challenge for the CNAs. I don't think they had the experience to manage him at first. I suggested how they could more successfully approach him to gain his cooperation. They appreciated my suggestions, which helped them become better caregivers.

Tom began picking up things that were lying around. He wandered into other residents' rooms and would take things. He might be found in someone else's bed. One day he saw some nuts and bolts on a table and he swallowed the nuts. I took him to the hospital for X-rays. Surgery wasn't called for and the doctor said, "This too shall pass."

I met with the administrator and expressed my concern about leaving things such as the nuts where residents could find them. I don't like to be a pain in the butt, but sometimes I felt I had to tell someone about potential risks or problems with care so that they could correct potential problems. I have a good relationship with staff so they listen to me.

I've talked to some caregivers who were upset about how their loved ones were treated. They expect the staff to treat them like mature adults, when they are more like children, who do childish things, for instance putting things in their mouths like steel nuts. I've observed that the staff have some days when it seems they are managing kindergarten rather than adults. They do treat residents with respect, but with certain behaviors they reacted with disrespect. They were dealing with the shell of a human being, not a person.

Tom was an easy-going man and Alzheimer's didn't change that. I was concerned when another male resident pushed and hit him. Tom had wandered into his neighbor's room who was probably defending his space. I found out later that his wife had told him to keep people out of his room. The problem increased; however, and he seemed to be targeting Tom and hitting him with his cane. I talked to the administration and they moved the other gentleman and monitored him more closely.

Soon after I placed Tom, I decided to take a break. It was winter, so I went to Arizona and spent time with friends and relatives. I missed sharing the time with Tom, but I soon relaxed and enjoyed visiting and seeing the sights. My spirit of adventure was beginning to resurface after having been submerged in the caregiver quagmire so long. I am so fortunate to have had the support I needed from my family, friends, and my support group. My heart is full of gratitude and I hope that I can be of encouragement to other struggling caregivers.

Roger's story continues:

Roger had been taking care of his wife at home for ten years. This was not just a brief rollercoaster ride, he was living on the rollercoaster hour after hour; day and night, without a way to get off. His emotions ran the gamut from joy to depression. When Betty Jo became afraid of him and called the police to have him arrested he was at wits end. How can you care for someone who is hysterically afraid of you? The answer came unexpectedly:

For five years the PACE program enabled me to care for Betty Jo at home. Otherwise she would have been in a nursing home. However, even with her having adult day care and I some respite, it became no longer safe for me to take care of her at home. She needed full time professional nursing care.

The day after she wandered into the frigid night, I was beside myself. I was a nervous wreck. I made an appointment to see my counselor. Betty Jo was at the Senior Community Center Day Care. While in counseling my cell phone rang and the caller ID showed it was my social worker, so I answered. He said, "Betty Jo's doctors, our PACE team, and the nursing home medical team and administration have agreed: "It's time."

I knew what he meant and asked, "What's the timeline?"

He answered, "Thirty minutes." I was stunned. They had already made all the arrangements for her to go to the nursing home. Paperwork had been completed when she was there for respite care. I gathered a suitcase full of Betty Jo's things that she would need for the next few days. I was in a dither but already beginning to feel some relief.

The PACE van took Betty Jo from the adult day care facility directly to the nursing home. They welcomed her and she walked right in without any resistance. I didn't go see her and left her clothes and things with a nurse. The director suggested that I not go in to see her for several days so that she could get used to the routine. That was good advice.

That first evening after I placed Betty Jo I felt relieved from the heavy burden that had defined me for so many years. It was a cold winter night, so I built a fire in the fireplace and looked up on the mantel. She had placed all her knick-knacks up there and I had no idea what they meant to her and they meant nothing to me. I knew she wouldn't be coming home again, so I went out to the garage and retrieved some of my knick-knacks such as my old fishing creel, landing net, bait box, an old fishing reel, minnow bucket, and antique lures. I placed my first fishing rod across the antlers of my trophy elk. I replaced her pictures with those of my own. I wasn't trying to put her out of my mind, but I guess I was feeling free to express the self that had been repressed for so long.

When I went in to see her the first time, she thought I was there to take her home. She had her suitcase packed. I told her that the doctor wanted her to stay and I couldn't violate doctor's orders. I learned early on to let the doctor be the bad guy. This approach did take the blame off me in her mind. I took the suitcase home to remove this mental trigger for her to leave.

After a few days she had lost all fear of me. She loved to see me, because she thought I was her ticket out. As time went by she became more demanding that I take her home. She tried to manipulate me with, "If you loved me you would take me home with you." Or "I promise to be a good girl. I won't cause any trouble." And she would cry. It almost broke my heart to leave her desperately begging and crying. Other times she tried the old guilt trip, "You brought me here to die didn't you." or "What did I do wrong that they put me in this prison?" This went on for nearly five years. I still went in to see her but repelled her pleas.

At first I absorbed her pain like a sponge. I felt so guilty about placing her and yet I knew she was where she needed to be. I knew down deep in my heart that I had been lovingly responsible.

Betty Jo settled into the routine of nursing home life rather quickly, which surprised me. She participated in activities and cooperated with staff. I heard very few complaints about her behavior. The staff engaged her and treated her as an individual by getting to know her. I had filled out another questionnaire about her past life, her likes and dislikes and from that information the nurses, CNAs and other staff could engage her in conversations.

Early on Betty Jo wanted books, but she couldn't understand what she was reading. That frustrated her, because she had taught reading to fourth graders. She felt like a failure. She lost track of time and when I'd go in she'd say, "You never come see me." So I bought her a diary and every time I went in I'd write in it what we did that day. Doing that made me feel better, but when I'd show her what was written, she'd say, "That proves it. You never come see me." Too much information; I had forgotten to validate her feelings.

I took her for drives in the nearby mountains and countryside. She loved to get out, but when she got tired she would say, “Take me home.” She meant back to the nursing home. Betty Jo’s incontinence got worse and after one embarrassing accident I didn’t take her anymore.

I became more comfortable when I went to visit. I stopped and talked to other residents. I shook hands with the men. One old rancher latched onto my cowboy hat. He wore it proudly. Maybe it reminded him of who he was. I told the nurse to let him wear it for a few days. I let another resident hold our little Maltese (Muffin) and the nurse said it was the first time she had ever seen her smile. After that I told her she had a beautiful smile and she just glowed. Those of us who had our loved ones in memory care got acquainted and joined in social activities, birthday and anniversary celebrations and we were just one big happy family.

I learned a lot by watching staff interact with residents. One man who had Alzheimer’s had been a psychiatrist. He followed a CNA while she took vital signs of the residents. At first I thought he was being a nuisance, but they gave him a pad and pencil and he would talk to each patient and write a prescription. That smart CNA found a way to help him feel important and valued. What she and others did in that regard helped reduce boredom and inappropriate behaviors throughout the memory care unit.

Betty Jo’s mental and physical condition deteriorated over the next five years. Toward the end we had a scheduled appointment with our doctor. He told me that she only had two weeks to live, because she had quit eating and drinking. I was not surprised. He asked if I had made final arrangements. By this time I had become more pragmatic and less emotional in my decision making. I had indeed decided with a funeral home a year before but never thought she would linger.

I notified her children that the end was near and I’d keep them posted. She had gone into a semi vegetative state so the staff, with my approval, moved her from memory care into the general population. She had been there a couple weeks when I went in one day and I found her sitting in her wheelchair and fully awake. She smiled as I walked up and she greeted me, “Hi Roger.” I was flabbergasted. She hadn't said my name in a couple of years. I asked her if she wanted to pet Muffin, and she said, "Yes." I was amazed that she spoke a word that I could understand.

There was a country-western-gospel group playing in the commons area and I asked her if she would like to go listen. She said, "Yes." I wheeled her into the room and she enjoyed the music. While they were singing a love song she turned to me and said, "I love you Alan." I got a little more than misty eyed. When they sang the closing song "How Great Thou Art" I turned to her and she was singing along. What an amazing day that was. There weren't many moments to cherish in those days but that was a big one.

I was amazed at her resilience. One day I walked into her room and she was lying down and she patted the bed and motioned for me to lie down next to her. She wanted to be loved on. I curled up next to her and she relaxed and fell asleep in my arms. It made me feel good knowing I was able to comfort her.

A week later I got the call that they wanted to put her back into memory care, because they caught her walking out the front door. Up to that time it had taken two CNAs to walk her to the bathroom! She went back to memory care and lived another 14 months, but she began that gradual decline that I was so familiar with. I was back on the emotional rollercoaster.

I updated Betty Jo's end-of-life directives several times. She was to have no heroic measures to prolong her life such as surgeries, hospitalization, antibiotics, oxygen and no feeding tube. She could have pain medication. We took her off some but not all her antianxiety medications. They still tried to make her eat and fed her with what I termed as 'industrial strength nutritional drinks' that kept her alive.

Had I known then what I know now, I would have directed that she be given food but not fed. It's personal with me, but I can't see prolonging life at the point when she was in the last stage of actively dying and having already suffered 16 years with dementia. It was hard to watch, but I knew it wouldn't be long.

The call came just as I was leaving Muffin to see Betty Jo. The nurse calmly and softly said, "Betty Jo just passed away." I said, "Thank you." and directed her to follow the instructions I had on file. I wasn't surprised or even stunned. I felt a wave of relief unlike any I have ever felt. I was relieved that Betty Jo was no longer suffering and had passed on to be with Jesus Christ, our Lord and Savior. I didn't go see her body. I remember her alive when I said my last goodbye and I still remember her that way. We all react differently to death which to me is very private. There is no proper way to deal with dying and death.

Even though I had lived alone for the past six years, I really wished that I had someone that evening to be with me. Death had finalized my caregiver journey and I was especially alone that evening. I didn't need someone to talk to as much as just having someone there. I really wanted to hug and be hugged. I'm glad I had Muffin. Her big brown eyes and the tilt of her head communicated understanding and sympathy. She slept next to me from that time on.

I had a deep sense of relief. I was free and I wasn't sad or didn't cry. Later I had moments of tears and I missed her. I have the satisfaction that I had been a good caregiver—not perfect—but I have no regrets. It was time for me to take my grief forward toward into new chapter in my life. *Alan's story continues in Chapter 6.*

Faye's story continues:

Faye had cared for Jake in the outback of the Colorado Rocky Mountains where there were few local resources to support home caregivers. The day came when Jake had a seizure and after he recovered, his doctor gave orders for him to go directly to a local nursing home. Life changed for both, but the rollercoaster ride for Faye was about to go off the rails: There's the old adage, "Cheer up things could be worse. So I cheered up and sure enough, things got worse:"

The nursing home was new, spacious, and clean. Jake was unaware of the change to his surroundings. As he recovered from his seizure, he became more difficult. I visited most days and I was disappointed with what I felt should have been better care. It seemed the staff was new and untrained to handle dementia cases. I complained first to the floor nurse and nothing changed. I talked to the administrator and still found no satisfaction. I contacted the regional ombudsman to intercede on my behalf. There was some improvement and although I wasn't totally satisfied, I felt that they were good caregivers and with more experience the staff would take better care of Jake.

It was about a year later when the nursing home administrator called and told me they were having more problems with Jake. He was wandering around and going into other residents' rooms and taking things. When confronted, he became defensive. The administrator told me that they could no longer have him in their facility. I contacted our regional ombudsman again and she tried to negotiate with them but to no avail. They checked with other nursing homes and couldn't find even one in the area that would take him. I was getting desperate.

The administrator told me that they found a facility 150 miles from my house. I was disappointed that there was no place closer. This meant having to drive over the Continental Divide on Wolf Creek Pass to the far southwestern corner of Colorado. To visit Jake in the winter would be risky and dangerous, because of avalanches and treacherous highway conditions. This was another one of those fall in your lap decisions over which I had no choice. I wasn't happy about it, but there was nothing I could do.

I was very apprehensive about all of this, because I had no control. The staffs of the two nursing homes coordinated Jake's transfer. It went so smoothly that Jake wasn't even aware that he had moved. Despite the greater distance, I felt better about his new home. From the very moment that we were greeted and I witnessed how the staff approached Jake, I felt relief.

I stayed overnight to finish the care plan, meet the staff, and tour the facility. I was pleasantly surprised that even in a rural area, this care center had a staff who was well trained in managing residents with Alzheimer's and other dementias. The campus was new and had some amenities including a massage therapist who helped Jake relax. I witnessed first-hand a CNA handling Jake when he was getting a little belligerent. She just validated his feelings and asked him if he would like to take her for a walk outside. He calmed down immediately.

I enjoyed the drive home back over the Divide and was the most relaxed I had been in several years. My anxiety level decreased and I didn't feel depressed. Even though I wouldn't be able to see Jake as often, I knew he was in a safe place and well taken care of. As for me I slowly regained my interests. I desperately missed Jake, but I was getting used to being alone. Won't be long until I'd be back in the saddle again (I thought.)

Then I got the call. It had happened again! I felt like I just got bucked off my horse and onto the rollercoaster. The administrator called and said that they wanted to transfer Jake, because he was causing problems like before. When they confronted him, he became combative. They just couldn't handle his behaviors and the families and caregivers of residents were complaining. Now what was I supposed to do? I was at the end of my rope and now I felt like they were threatening to cut the rope I was holding onto. I was beyond desperate.

I was expecting a discharge notice, but about a week later the social worker called and said that the doctor had increased some of Jake's medication and it was calming him down and if that trend continued they would keep him.

After not seeing Jake during the winter months, COVID-19 guidelines confined us with "Stay at Home" and nursing home visitor restrictions for another four months. It did spare me the 150 mile drive over the Divide, but it was frustrating and sad. The facility sent detailed weekly letters and provided a COVID hot line with 24/7 updates. CNAs showed Jake family photos and he would smile. However, he wasn't aware that I hadn't been there to see him. I felt some degree of relief knowing he was in good hands and am getting more used to the situation that I have no control over anyway. Things are actually turning out rather well for me, but I still grieve losing him.

The Forest View

When you become an advocate you join your loved one's care team. Some of your teammates are doctors, nurses, CNAs, therapists, nutritionists and other front-line health care folks. You also coordinate with outside providers like your loved one's doctor or hospice.

When you ask for an update, you may hear different things from different staff. Some want to comfort you with good news. Others want to give you the unvarnished truth. Some see you as part of the team others think you are in the way; even secretly blaming you for the bad shape your loved one is in. Some have years of experience and others are new to the job. Administrators eventually weed out the bad ones and do their best to hire qualified staff.

Good administrators provide continuing education for their employees. You are not just an observer; you are a proactive influence on all these folks and work alongside of them. You become a negotiator, a bridge builder, a cheerleader, and a problem solver. You do all you can to help them succeed.

Newly placed love ones are in unfamiliar surroundings and are attended by strangers. Other residents may be intimidating or won't even talk to your loved one. You are on edge as well. You still want to be in charge and it may seem that you have been kicked to the curb. You may be advised to not visit for a while, so your loved one can settle in. It's true that every time you visit, you are a reminder of home and a trigger to get out of there. We've all heard things like, "I don't like it here. Take me home." It may be good advice to stay away for a while, but it can seem like a slap in the face. It's like leaving your baby with a babysitter for the first time and you aren't there to oversee care. These are not 16-year-old babysitters; they are professionals who are with compassion and firmness when necessary.

Be cautious about believing everything your loved one tells you. A demented loved one may claim of being abused, and starved. If they haven't already learned the art of manipulation, they will develop it into a fine art. Remember, you are dealing with a diminished person. Talk to the staff about what your loved one says about you. Try this, "I won't believe half of what I hear about you if you won't believe half of what you hear about me."

Once you place someone, it usually takes time to establish trust with staff. Caregivers and families have certain expectations and if those aren't met, conflict can arise. Communication is paramount. Asking questions is more effective than making demands.

Compliment the good and positive things you see them doing. Thank individuals for their good work whenever you can. If a soft approach doesn't work at first, become firmer.

Care conferences help you develop relationships with department heads that are usually more cooperative than adversarial. Get the staff perspective on your loved one's condition and share your feelings about what is working and what is not.

Each state has its own regulations about how often care conferences must be held. Most are quarterly, unless your approval is required for something new. You will receive calls for significant changes and accidents like a fall. If your loved one is competent, he or she must be allowed to attend the scheduled conferences. If you would like to talk without your loved one, ask for an additional conference.

Like a doctor's appointment, you will be well served to prepare and make notes about what you want to ask and say. You may want to speak first at the meeting to direct staff to your concerns. It also shows you are engaged and want to make the most of the session. Ask questions whenever they are on your mind. If you are not satisfied with how your care conferences are run, speak to the facility director.

Chapter 6

Grieve: I Remember and adjust to a new life

Grief is a human experience through which we *learn* from what was, *adjust* to what is, and to *imagine* what can be. We all grieve in our own way. Cultures have different rituals and individuals have different experiences and relationship with what was lost. Your grief will continue after you lose your loved one. You will remember all you have experienced and have learned. It takes time to adjust to a life without him or her. Take your time.

In the early phases of caregiving you might not have thought much about what life would be like after your loved one dies. If you did, you felt guilty. You were mostly consumed with carrying the weight of your burden. You also grieved the loss of your loved one all along the way. You wept, were angry, felt sad, and rejected. You said goodbye so many times. When your loved one's final breath was taken, his or her journey was over but yours was not.

Most long-term caregivers feel some relief. You may accept death as beneficial, knowing that of your loved one's suffering has ended. You most likely will feel released from the burden as well.

Death at the end of such a long journey was anticipated, but it is still a shock. Luckily, you may have the chance to be near when death comes. Dying is such a profound part of life. There is a comfort that comes from being present and witnessing death.

At the same time, your grieving continues. You must adjust to brand new reality. The finality of being alone is strange. The structure of your daily routine is gone and that may give you a disoriented feeling. You may not know what to do next.

You will always remember the person: your shared experiences, challenges, accomplishments, laughs, joy and sadness. What your loved one taught you, both good and bad has changed you. You want to remember to be able to carry the memories and lessons forward. The passing of time will mellow the unpleasant memories. You have the power to put them in an imaginary box on a closet shelf. You may pull the box down and revisit if you choose, but you don't have to keep the hurt in you all the time. You have the power to discard hurtful memories and take them out of the box.

Your friends may give you advice that doesn't help. Those who have never been caregivers may tell you how you should grieve. Much of it doesn't make sense to you. Some people expect you to grieve in the way they do. Perhaps, they say "I'm so sorry for your loss," or "I know this is very hard time for you." You may even not be sad. You might even feel guilty because you think you should be sadder than you are. They may say, "She's in a better place" and it upsets you because you aren't. It may be exciting or scary or both at the same time.

You will make mistakes and find unexpected pleasures. You may jump into things or go very slowly. It's your call. You get to grieve how you want to grieve. Slough off unwanted advice. Try new things in small pieces. If you enjoy it, do more; if you don't, do less. It would be a mistake to buy an around-the-world cruise and get to the first port and learn that you don't like cruising!

Over time your grief will subside, but it is likely to recur, triggered by holidays, anniversaries, a smell, a photograph. It's natural that some things take you back. Even though your feelings may be upsetting, it is valuable to renew your grief. It helps you remember. A glance in the rearview mirror now and then will give you a clearer understanding of where you were and where you are now.

Caregiving responsibilities no longer restrict what you can do. This is the time to renew your thinking and move forward to another chapter in your life. You sacrificed yourself to be a caregiver and now is the time to renew friendships, go places, and do things. What activities and relationships did you give up? What are some things you've never been able to do? Dare to be outrageous.

You have reached the summit of your caregiver journey and there is a whole new world in front of you. There is no parking lot at the summit, only a viewpoint where you can pause. Take a deep breath and begin to enter your new life.

Grieve: Remember and adjust to a new life

Ted-Just a closer walk with Thee
Charlotte-I'm moving forward
Roger-Passing on what was given to me
Linda-I'm going fishing
Mary-I'm living life to the fullest
Rosa-I got more than a gold star
Martin-I'm glad I didn't try to do it alone
Fred-I found a new passion
The Forest View

Ted's story concludes

Ted was a loving and faithful husband who took care of his wife for as long as he could. He struggled, joined a support group, made a caregiving plan, got resources to take care of Flo for as long as possible at home, but if the day came that he could no longer care for her at home, he was prepared to place her into a nursing home. He continued to be her advocate and worked with the staff to make sure she had the care she needed. He looks back with no regrets and moves forward.

I was so relieved that I had been able to enroll Flo into our PACE program. I know that some caregivers have had some unpleasant experiences with having their loved one living in a nursing home, but my experience was a very good one. The administration and nursing staff gave my wife the best of attention and care. It wasn't perfect, but I have to say it was excellent.

When I first placed Flo that first night I was so alone. I felt a loss as if she were dead. Yet the journey hadn't ended. As the days past and I visited her, I began to feel detached from her. I didn't want her to die and yet I honestly wished the Lord would take her to heaven and her agony, as well as mine, would be over

Toward the end Flo couldn't say much, but she whispered to me that she was afraid of death, wondering what was ahead. I've not been one to share my faith in God, but to comfort her I told her what I believe. I told her in simple terms that I believed there is a God of the universe who loves us even though we sin against Him. He sent Jesus Christ His son, to earth. He died on a cross as a sacrifice for our sins and God promised that if we accept His sacrifice and believe, He will save us to be with Him for eternity in heaven. I asked her if she would do that. She thought about it and looked at me and with a smile on her face said, "Yes. I believe."

Her doctor came in soon after examining her. He said that she only had a couple days to live and that I had better call the family together. Our families were scattered across the country, but many came to see Flo before she died. I was a little apprehensive since I had been the brunt of a lot of abuse.

When Flo's kids came, just the little time they spent with us was a life-changing experience for all of us. We were together as family. I held Flo's hand and softly assured her that I was okay and that it was okay for her to: "Go lie down in green pastures with the Lord." She took only a few shallow breaths, exhaled her last, and passed on to be with God. I was finally at peace. That experience changed all of us. My faith in God is stronger than ever. I learned later that one of the children even started going to church. That meant a lot to me.

It was time to move forward with my life, but I had been living from day to day for years with little thought ever given to life after caregiving. Flo's passing left a void in my life that I didn't know how to fill, but I'm not one to just sit around, so I gave it a lot of thought. I didn't have to feel guilty anymore about doing the things that I have always enjoyed. I even thought about doing something that I never thought I'd be able to do. I started playing golf again and I went fishing with an old fishing buddy. The RV had been sitting idle for five years but now I'm going to hit the road and see America and go north into Canada. I'm not used to traveling alone, so that is going to take some adapting. I'll probably be talking to Flo as though she were in the seat next to me and that'll be fine because I'm okay now.

Charlotte's story concludes

Charlotte's husband had a long battle with Parkinson's disease. She cared for him for 15 years. The first few years he lived a normal life, but then the tremors began. Doctors were able to prescribe medicines that helped for a time, but eventually quit working. As his disease progressed, her caregiving load became overwhelming. She joined a support group and put together a care team for herself and Carl. He died peacefully in a local nursing home under hospice care. Charlotte moved forward with her life.

When Carl passed on I honestly felt relieved. I was glad that I no longer had to deal with the stress and glad for him that his struggles were over. My stepdaughters had come from out of state to help with the funeral and helped me get my house and life reorganized. They mirrored those thoughts of relief as well. I feel that I was grieving for Carl way before he passed, so now I try to think of more pleasant days from our life together whenever I think of him.

Living alone has many up sides, but the house felt much too empty. Carl and I had always had animals and I was devastated when our dog died two weeks after Carl passed. My stepdaughter encouraged me to get a pet. I went to the animal shelter and adopted a kitten (Jesse James) and a dog (Bandit). They are both great company and when I take Bandit for a walk, I get the added benefit of visiting with neighbors who are walking their dogs.

One of the most difficult things that I dealt with during the latter stages of Carl's slide was the constant worry when I left the house. Even though I was fortunate to have home health care for him while I was gone, he was always foremost on my mind. It was definitely a relief to not have that concern after he passed. I felt guilty about those feelings until I talked them through with a counselor as well as my caregiver support group.

For the last two years of his struggle with Parkinson's, I was unable to travel to see other family members. So, taking those trips were at the top of the list after he passed. One trip was particularly gratifying because it gave me a chance to reconnect with my sister in Florida after many years. We now stay in touch regularly. I visited friends and family in New Mexico who have since come to visit me.

My stepdaughter moved here from Virginia not long after Carl's passing. It has been wonderful having her close by, as well as my grandson who moved here about a year ago.

I've had fun showing my daughter and grandson the Rocky Mountains. I've gotten to know them better. My life just keeps getting more exciting. I just received an invitation to my other grandson's wedding next spring. It is a great feeling to know that there is nothing preventing me from attending and enjoying a worry-free visit.

I can now enjoy playing more tennis again as well as having coffee or lunch with friends and not have those caregiving worries on my mind. In addition to my tennis activities, I have joined the Friends of the Library Board. Having the time and freedom to serve on the board has been gratifying. Of course, there are moments of reflection about my 37 years with Carl, but most often I choose to remember the good times we had camping, fishing and traveling together.

Roger's story concludes

Roger took care of his wife for sixteen years. They were able to travel some at first, and the dementia was only a little upsetting. Her condition deteriorated and Roger took care of her at home for the first 10 years and was her advocate for six years after she was placed into a nursing home. He had lived on an emotional rollercoaster, grieving her loss all that time. When Betty Jo passed on he felt no sadness, only a wave of relief as if released from a prison.

I arranged a memorial rather than a funeral service. Funerals are too gloomy. Most people really didn't know Betty Jo. She was an amazing woman. Professionally, she was a masterful schoolteacher, who specialized in teaching reading skills to elementary students. She was an adventurous woman, having rafted the Colorado River through the Grand Canyon. Betty Jo was active in her church, singing in the choir, teaching Sunday school, and helping with other service to her community. Remembering is part of grieving. It is not letting go but holding on to precious memories. Betty Jo's son read the eulogy that included not only the positive side of her life but also how she had battled depression all her adult life.

My love for Betty Jo never waned during our 21 years together. I loved without expectation or expressions of being loved in return. I had gradually become withdrawn from her when she no longer responded to my presence. The dementia had changed our relationship. I was very alone and socially detached. I am a social person. I recharge my batteries when I am around people. I had missed that for so many years.

I had been so consumed with my day to day routine of caring for her that I had given up most of my hobbies and interests. Dementia made a shell of both of us.

Just a month before her death I left for a vacation. I had planned the road trip months before. I had always enjoyed driving cross-country seeing America, but this trip had something special. It was the first time that I had gone on a long trip without her. There were so many sights along the way that I wanted to share, but I felt even more alone. Along the route however, I had friends and relatives to see and soon I relaxed and enjoyed the trip.

One of the greatest blessings has been that I have been drawn closer to my stepfamily. Although we are scattered and seldom see each other, we are in contact and that means a lot to me.

One of the things I missed in the last phase of my journey was being able to converse with a woman. I wasn't interested in romance, just having some female companionship. I love to go four-wheeling in our nearby mountains, so I invited some widows to go "Jeeping" with me. They all had enjoyed Jeeping with their husbands in the high country and we found a common bond in sharing the trails.

All of us were grieving the loss of our spouses but riding the old mining and stagecoach roads brought back good memories. It was even more meaningful that we could continue to enjoy a small but important part of our lives with friends. It's fruitless to forget, so why not enjoy opening a new chapter of life with others. It sure beats sitting around moping!

My caregiving experiences changed me in positive ways. I am more patient and less judgmental of others. I learned that everyone has a life story that brought them to the place where they are now.

Having survived my caregiver years, I can listen with greater empathy to others who are facing the caregiver journey. I can offer answers to some of their questions and encourage them to avoid the mistakes I made and let them know I understand the feelings that go with caregiving. What good is it to have survived an ordeal and never share how you got through it?

Linda's story concludes

Linda followed through on her commitment to take care of their mother toward the end of her life. She took advantage of local resources that enabled her to take care of her mom at home. She never had to go to a nursing home. The journey was rough at times, but they finished the course.

I planned the first vacation I had in more than five years. It was the first thing that I did to take care of myself without feeling selfish. I needed a getaway and I was confident that mom was well taken care of. I had a wonderful time and was on the way home when I received the news that mom had passed. Her death was expected, but I thought it was some time in the future. I was surprised and yet not really.

I wanted to be home but it was another day's drive. It's amazing that God protected me during mom's passing. It was really good that I wasn't there. If I had been with her, I would likely have micro-managed. That would have caused me high anxiety and stress that I didn't need.

I postponed mom's memorial service. My life after mom passed was like an empty nest. For days I found myself saying, "What do I do today?" I didn't realize how much time I had spent thinking about mom. Either I was trying to make her life better in some special way or just doing the mundane chores of hourly caregiving. Regardless, my whole life had been focused on mom. I have no regret about that. It's been nearly nine months since she passed. I still come across items that remind me of a situation I tried to make better for her.

I've had an opportunity to talk to someone else who was going through what I went through with mom and it reminded me of all the things I did to help her. It also made me feel good to be able to listen to someone else with the understanding that I had received from my support group. Listening to a struggling caregiver gave additional purpose to my experiences.

Mom and I didn't always have the best of relationships. Being her caregiver gave me a chance to be there for her when she needed me the most. Looking back now is hard, but I'm grateful for the experience and feel God blessed me with that responsibility.

After mom passed and I got her estate settled, I gave my brother his half of mom's estate. We cried together and without saying the words, the past was forgiven in each of our hearts. We are brother and sister again. I don't have any long-range plans, but for now, I'm going fishing.

Mary's story concludes

Mary cared for her husband David who had been in declining health and had dementia. He was uncooperative and difficult to manage. He never was so sick or immobile that she needed to place him into a care facility, but she stayed with him until he died at home. Mary started living again:

I took care of David for ten years, putting my own life on hold. I did a lot of reading during those years, but found I could rarely go out to do things with friends. It was a lonely and an unfulfilling life except for the care I lovingly gave him.

After he died, I settled into learning to live alone and to find out what I wanted to do with the rest of my life. I began to meditate daily and found great solace and peace of mind in this discipline. I also began to take very good care of myself--starting right after he died.

I began eating healthy food and started to do Tai Chi and Nordic walking. I traveled and visited old friends and former students. I took up water color painting, played the piano, gardening, sang in a choral group, and entertained old friends and made new ones.

One of the major things I did was to start writing about my very interesting life. As my lifestyle became more active, I lost 70 pounds and went from a size 22 to a 14--back to what I wore when I was first married.

I had gotten to know a man who had worked for me years before. He lost his apartment and had no place to live--and so I invited him to live with me. We became very close friends--he is like a son to me. We played music together, camped, went for walks and to the beach, and talked. He continues to live with me and says he will always be there for me. I'm 82 years young and it's good to have a strong man looking after my yard, home, and me.

I have to say I very much like the 'new' me that I have created. People tell me I look radiant, happy and about 55 or 60 years old. I have not been sick in 30 years and I attribute this to my positive attitude about life, my active lifestyle, and ability to deal with stress. I enjoy life totally and look forward to many more years of good health, creativity and new friendships. I am blessed to have family close by, my housemate, and many students from my teaching years who care about me, visit me, call me and help me out. My life after the death of my husband of 60 years is full to the brim and I am content and fortunate.

Rosa's story concludes

Rosa was her parent's caregiver. She was very close to her father but always felt abused by her mother. After her father died, she continued to be her mother's caregiver and advocate.

As a child, I watched many old movies late into the night with my mother. I felt that if I kept her company, it would somehow keep her from getting drunk. (It didn't). Many of the old films we watched would have a tear-jerking death scene in which, during the last moments of the character's life, he or she would be surrounded by loved ones proclaiming their love or would have those final moments to reconcile any past emotional wounds. Music would swell, tears would flow and final words would make everything right and good. Then the loved one would gently close her eyes and slip away.

Over the next few decades I continued to try to save my mother. I don't know if it was my selfish hope to be her savior or if I could navigate thru the emotional pain to truly be an authentic force of love and change in her life. Later my counselor told me that she had a "narcissistic personality." I was intrigued. I spent time learning about this disorder and its effects on the family of a narcissist. The understanding that I acquired helped me realize that I would likely never receive love or praise or appreciation and would never be able to have a healthy mother-daughter relationship.

As a caregiver for both my parents I basked in the appreciation and love my father bestowed on me. It was a privilege and an honor to be his caregiver. My mother, on the other hand, was viciously mean. Nothing was good enough in assisted living. When she required full-time care in a long-term facility the staff heard relentlessly that I had stolen their money, physically abused her, given her clothing away, etc. Nothing was acceptable to her. She blamed me for her misery. Interestingly, I saw staff tending to her and she embraced them and told how much she loved them.

As I sat with my Mother during the last three days of her life, she was seldom coherent or alert. On her final dying day she had a window of alertness. She had some rambling thoughts of her childhood. During one coherent time she looked at me and called my name and gazed into my eyes. Her words to me were clear. She said, "I always knew you were beautiful. I just didn't know how beautiful you'd be." Then, she studied my face and clearly said, "I've always loved you," and those were her final words.

I had journaled during the three-day vigil at her bedside. I poured out all the feelings and struggles I had with my mom. As a professional nurse and recovering alcoholic I recalled how mom told so many people that she loved them. How she ended phone calls with her friends by telling them she loved them. Why didn't she tell me before now? These thoughts were honest and stark and painful. Even at this end-of-life time I felt that perhaps the movie's final scene would play out and all would be lovely. But I didn't get the "gold star" of appreciation. I acknowledged her dying words.

I put her final words, two short sentences, on the bottom of the six pages of journal entries. Those two simple sentences, such small little sentences, would have been so meaningful to me through the years. It might have been the best she could do. Yet for me it did not produce forgiveness and forgetting. The emotional scars were too engrained; the scars now have their place and have become manageable. But still I can't make sense of it.

My greatest reward is that I gave of myself to care for my parents. My "gold star" is within me knowing I did my very best. I do not let the past determine how I feel and live. I am a better person now. I can continue to celebrate and to be uplifted by the love-bearing people in my life. My loving father, the joy-giving children and grandchildren, the grief-supporting fellow travelers, an amazing loving partner and the simple joy of being loved by many family and friends are my rewards.

Martin's story

Martin and Trina had been married 55 years when she was diagnosed with dementia. He took care of her all by himself for five years as she followed the downward path. Instead of placing her into a nursing home, Martin hired a small staff of CNAs to provide the care that he could no longer provide. She lived at home only a short time but seemed content and he felt satisfied and good about his decision.

I was fortunate to find a caregiver support group early on and learned from their experiences things that worked for me. It was comforting for me to be able to share my frustrations and bounce ideas around the group to get their perspectives.

Trina passed away ten years after she was diagnosed. I was her 24/7 caregiver for four years. She was not difficult for me to care for, because she couldn't talk, walk, feed herself, or do anything disruptive. She would go to sleep about eight o'clock at night and sleep all night until eight o'clock the next morning. I was able to get my rest all that time.

Hospice was with us for over a year and along with our caregivers, they certainly helped prepare me for Trina's passing. My period of grieving has been short-lived, because there were so many times during the terminal illness that I grieved losing her. I said goodbye many times.

My state of mind when she passed was one of relief for her and for me. She had no quality of life and no prospect of ever getting better. I'm so glad that I didn't try to take care of Trina by myself. I had found others who wanted to help and I made sure they knew how to do what I asked them to do for us.

I have moved forward and I'm happy and well. I miss Trina and always will, but I'm not one to sit around and mope. I meet with some other widowers for breakfast each morning and that gets the day off to a good start. Keeping busy is important to me. I have a lady friend whom I have known for over 50 years and we enjoy doing things together. Life is good.

Fred's store concludes

Fred was a faithful husband and caregiver. He had struggled like all caregivers, but he persevered to the very end. He handled Bridget's death in a very unusual manner.

I knew that the Bridget's diagnosis would lead to her death, but I thought it was a long way off, so I didn't think about it often. I didn't worry about my life after her death either. I concentrated on how to cope with what remained of her life. I even thought her prognosis of dementia was a life sentence for me. I was 67 at the time and she could have lived for 20 years, so I might die first.

The trigger that got me to seriously think more about her death came in an unusual way. At the end of a rather routine caregiver conference in the memory care unit, a hospice representative slid over a brochure. The title was *Signs of Active Dying*. I thought it was a stark and impersonal way to get the message that Bridget could die soon.

I read the brochure and was put off by the grim picture of agonal breathing - the gasping for air and long periods of not inhaling and thrashing around as if in great pain. I initially decided I didn't want any part of it. But, it did make me focus on the need to plan for the end; I didn't want to be unprepared.

I went to a counselor who specializes in end-of-life planning. He opened my mind to see the end of life differently. Even though Bridget was unable to communicate and seemed almost comatose, I could catch a facial expression and even a smile occasionally. I wanted to be there for her, to comfort her, and witness her death. I read about rituals from many cultures for aiding the dying and preparing the body. I developed a plan for music and things of comfort for her. Hearing is one of the last things to go and I thought that whether she hears or not, I wanted to do what I could to comfort her. I'm so glad I did make an end of life plan. It was a wonderful experience for me and I hope for her.

The hospice nurse called and said there seemed to be a change in Bridget. I went to visit immediately and noticed she was sleeping comfortably and not moving at all. I visited her for two more days and saw her serenely at peace. She was obviously in the process of actively dying.

We moved her to a special private room equipped by hospice to be a quiet place for someone near death and for family. I brought things she would find comforting and spent the rest of the day with her. I got the call the morning after we moved her. She had died during the night. I wished I would have been there for at that moment of death, but that wasn't to be.

One takes solace in the smallest things; I was pleased she died peacefully and quickly. I spent an hour with her alone, talking about our life and reading to her. I read the poem *"A Cup of Christmas Tea"*, which always makes me cry. It helped.

After my quiet time with her, I called for help to prepare the body. We washed her from head to foot and I rubbed on fragrant oil. Seeing her emaciated, bruised body made me wonder how she'd lived so long. Going through this helped me accept that she was gone. Few would do what I did. We completed our work and I donated the body to science.

Some senior care places try to avoid the reality of death. They may want the public to feel that they have only people who are full of life. Some even hide the body from view until no one is looking before moving it to a funeral home. I prefer a place that acknowledges and respects death as a sacred part of life.

After we had Bridget's body prepared, the nursing home had a ritual called "Arms of Angels." The body is slowly taken out on a gurney with family walking alongside. The staff and residents who desire, line the halls and stand silently in respect while music is playing. The staff often gets very close to the residents and grieve. It was a way for them to say, "Goodbye."

My strongest emotion since her death has been relief and feeling released from my caregiver burden; I am released from my prison of putting Bridget first. I can begin to rebuild my life. The prison door opened and I walked out into a different world from the one I had been living in. I no longer had restraints, schedules, and responsibilities. I was free indeed!

Of course, I had begun to try new things without her, but a part of me said I couldn't move on yet; I had to wait until death. There seemed to me no rational reason for that, but I couldn't let go emotionally when she was alive.

I do not feel the intense sadness that I have had for the loss of other family members. I have not cried since I read to Bridget's body. I imagine the long journey, the ambiguous grieving along the way, and our up-and-down relationship help me cope with her death.

It has been important to me to relive the important events we shared with each other. I don't live in the past, but I acknowledge what we gave to each other and I take the good stuff into my future. I've revisited the significant hurts and failures now and understand them better. Everything that happened in the past has brought me to where I'm now, but it is not the dominant force in my future.

Bridget's life-long anxiety made her high-maintenance and that robbed her of having empathy for me. I never felt my love was reciprocated. My feelings led to blaming. However, I chose to marry her, so I'm part of the deal. A counselor once asked why I married Bridget. I blurted out, "because she was beautiful, she would have me, and I really wanted to get out of my parent's house." We were not well-suited and I chose to marry when I was immature. I came to not blame her and accepted that I made a poor decision when I was very young. I could let that go. I could focus on the good things we built and the successes we enjoyed. I could move on.

I am proud that I have done my best. I have grown a lot, as we may do by overcoming big challenges: I am less afraid of growing older, more patient with people, and more confident I can overcome new hurdles.

When I divide my life into chapters, each begins with an event that has opened a new horizon. I have found a passion to help other caregivers. I have been given the opportunity to better choose what is good for me. I've become the person I want to be.

As a volunteer for Area Agency on Aging Advisory Council, I attended meetings of professional caregivers for seniors: nurses, social workers, hospice people, and medical staff. At one meeting I noticed that almost all of them were women. It occurred to me that if I were looking for a companion, this would be a good place to look. After enjoying the moment I put the thoughts aside; I'm married and a caregiver for a terminally ill wife. There might be time for that later but much later. If you are a romantic, you might imagine what came next.

I was in a meeting of a different sort and a woman intrigued me. We met for coffee and talked effortlessly. We became soul mates and now live together. So, grief after death did not include a rudderless searching for what is next. I'm eager to embrace it. As strange as it is to say, Bridget's diagnosis propelled me into a new chapter in my life that is wonderful.

The Forest View

Dementia, other neurological diseases, and old age make caregiver grief unique. The caregiver journey is very long, so caregivers wear out along the way. The losses are ambiguous, because your loved one comes and goes. He or she may be good at hiding the decline in public, only to melt down when you get home. Death is way off in the future. Caregivers may even have thoughts that they will die before their loved one does.

Caregiver grief is not well understood in western culture. Those who have experienced it have a different understanding than people who haven't. A loved one grieves over failing to remember, being unable to read or getting lost. You were saddened the first time you witnessed your loved one 'losing it' and you grieved that loss too.

Caregiver grief is often disenfranchised, that is, not recognized. Yes, others can imagine how stressful caregiving is, but many do not see the impact as you watch your loved one slowly die. Most people identify grief only with death and therefore you can't be grieving when your loved one is still breathing. Even caregivers themselves may not understand why they feel awful. Caregivers who try to fix the disease get really frustrated; they can't ever win. Remember, 'You can't stop it; you can't change it; you can't fix it.'

In almost every story you have read, caregivers feel lonely and isolated. We sometimes are rejected by those we need most. You feel you were losing yourself trying to do a job that can't be done. Your own future is held hostage because you are committed to caring. You became depressed more by the isolation and loneliness than the physical labor.

We adjust to many changes in life, such as when a dreaded meeting is cancelled and we stay home. These adjustments are easy. Others are profound and life changing. Take your time to adjust. You will get through it.

There is another change in your life; you have lost your job! You may feel your purpose is gone now that you are no longer a caregiver. What do you do with all that time that was spent caregiving! There may be ambivalence with grief; you may feel sad and pleased at the same time. That's okay, because both feelings have merit. Don't feel forced to choose one feeling over another. As time goes on you will find a new balance.

Just as some friends drew close and supported and some grew cold and distant, the future will also bring different reactions from friends. Imagine a bowl of marbles in which each marble is a person in your life. Some are near you and others are more distant. When your loved one's marble is removed, all the remaining marbles shift. They shift in relation to your marble and to the nearby marbles. As you adjust, your marble will move, too. That may cause other marbles to move closer or farther away. You will even find new marbles and fit them into the pile, causing more shifting. You and everyone around you will adjust repeatedly.

Grieving does not mean we need to leave the good memories behind. We do not need to 'get over it'. We do not need to 'move on'. We can remember what we had and cherish it. If a friend moves away we still laugh when we remember the fun we had. Our deceased parents had great influence on us. Why would we want to forget the blessings?

We don't need to endlessly relive the hurts, because we can edit our memories and keep the lessons. Those who have passed away can live in our memories as well as in the memories of those who knew them. Reach out to friends to share stories about your many meaningful experiences with your loved one. Appreciate how he or she touched others and was a part of their lives. In a real sense your loved one will always be with you. "You can let your loved one go and keep the love."

In the days following the final breath, use the time to pull over in a rest stop. This is a time to reflect. Most of us need a break to let the air out of the emotional balloon. Stay in the rest stop as long as you want. Then use it as a launching pad to move to new experiences and the exciting journey of the rest of your life.

Conclusion

Caring for another person is one of the highest callings that you will ever have. There is no greater love than caring for another person unto death. You are dedicated to a purpose beyond yourself.

At first it doesn't seem like much of a sacrifice, because loved ones are still highly functioning and the backpack is not heavy. Life is normal for the most part, but atypical behaviors begin to creep in.

The time comes when behaviors get more difficult. Like a worsening toothache, the pain cannot be ignored. The short-term memory gets worse and as certain portions of the brain begin to fail, so do some abilities to function. Some things go dreadfully wrong and your stress shoots up.

A neurologist conducts memory tests. Hearing words such as Mild Cognitive Impairment, dementia or Parkinson's is devastating. Fear and a feeling of hopelessness grip your soul. The initial shock wears off in time. Grieving your loss of dreams and plans together creates a void that makes life seem hollow.

You don't understand all the ramifications of the disease. You learn all you can by reading and attending seminars and workshops. Understanding the disease helps some, however it doesn't provide the skills you will need. Is there anything that can be done to slow down or cure the disease? How long does he or she have to live? What about me and my future? The answers are unclear, because science hasn't figured it out yet and every person's situation is different. There is no 'one size fits all' answer.

You begin to experience emotional and physical stress. Your burden becomes heavier. There is almost no time for yourself. Anger is one of the early signs of stress and grief. It isolates you and takes away part of who you are. Just as your loved one blames you, so you blame your loved one for their behaviors and loss of memories. Fear leads to blaming, criticism, and rejection.

The weight of the caregiver burden gets heavier and heavier on this long road. You wait until a crisis before you seek help. Family members are often the first ones a caregiver turns to, but they may not provide all the support you need.

Sometimes you just need to talk to someone. You may talk to a professional counselor to get beyond unresolved feelings and to restore balance. You may find compassion in caregiver support group.

The long journey continues through the phases of caring for your loved one. The hope for a cure or even slowing the progression isn't realistic and it seems hope is lost. Hope isn't lost, but reality changes what you hope for. We adjust to those changes and do all we can to make our loved one comfortable. We agonize over end-of-life directives and finances. It's good to make plans, but the best made plans don't cover all the bases. We don't know the future.

You may not place your loved one into a skilled nursing facility. Many die at home under the care of family and hospice. In rare circumstances a caregiver dies first.

Depending on the disease, body organs begin to fail. The doctor says the end is near when signs of active dying appear. Family and friends are called to the bedside to say their final goodbyes. How you handle the death depends on the texture of the relationship and your feelings about death. Some want to be there to share a sacred moment. Others don't want to be in the room. You can't hold others to your expectations. You have grieved their loss since you became aware that life was at risk.

When death arrives, your journey is over, but your grief continues. You are at a summit with a whole new horizon in front of you. You will grieve and remember the past. You will transition to a new life, a new way of seeing the world.

Unencumbered by the caregiving responsibility there is little holding you back. Now is the time to renew relationships that have been neglected.

In all these caregiver stories, not a single person failed to give the best care they were capable of. You will too.

Glossary

AAA – Area Agency on Aging is a federal and state funded program that provides a variety of resources to seniors. AAA provides counseling, home-care assistance, meals, transportation, respite care and more. Search online for Area Agency on Aging in your state and county.

Adult Day Care — professional adult care for adults with physical or mental diseases and disabilities. They provide short-term supervision. Caregivers get relief to care for themselves.

Adult Protective Services – County Health and Human Services administers protection for people who cannot protect themselves. They help people of abuse and neglect.

Advance Directives see also Five Wishes -- written instructions about medical procedures that a person does not want to be used at the end of life. For instance, CPR, feeding tubes, antibiotics or surgery.

Alzheimer's disease – a disease of the brain that is known mostly for causing memory loss, physical decline and death. It is the leading cause of dementia. The Alzheimer's Association provides publications, workshops, and programs that support patients and caregivers. Its primary mission is to fund research that leads to a cure. Visit alz.org

Ambiguous Loss -- A kind of significant loss in which the loved one is physically absent but psychologically present or is physically present but psychologically absent. People with a long-term terminal illnesses and old age slowly decline and lose functions, with periods of clarity and plateaus with ambiguous changes. Caregivers grieve each loss, sometimes deeply and sometimes with acceptance.

Anosognosia -- When someone rejects a diagnosis of mental illness, it's tempting to say that he's in denial. But someone with acute mental illness may not be thinking clearly enough to be aware that anything is wrong. They may instead have a lack of awareness. The medical term for this medical condition is anosognosia (pronounced ah.no.sog.NO.sha), from the Greek meaning "to not know".

Anticipatory Grief --- One of the first kinds of before-death grief to be described. We grieve for an expected death. Because it has been around a long time, many call any loss before death "anticipatory". It is better to use the term only when death is imminent. Caregivers often grieve well before death, as the loved one loses personhood and function. Caregivers also grieve for the loss of their own future and the loss of their quality of life.

Assisted Living Facility —A facility for people with disabilities and adults who cannot or who choose not to live independently.

Caregiver Burden – A medical term for the health effects of caregiving, including emotional stress, and physical exhaustion. It can cause elevated blood pressure, weight gain, excessive use of alcohol and emotional turmoil and depression.

Chronic Disease — a condition lasting more than a year that requires ongoing medical treatment or limits the ability to care for oneself.

CNA (Certified Nursing Assistant) - a person trained to perform nursing duties under the supervision of a registered nurse or doctor.

Comorbidity – the presence of more than one disorder in a person. Having multiple disorders complicates treatment and may worsen the outcome.

Dementia – a condition in which a person loses the ability to carry out daily tasks. It is a result of several specific diseases such as Alzheimer's, Parkinson's, or other neurological disorders. The specific symptoms depend on the disease but often manifest themselves in memory loss, mobility dysfunction, and hallucination.

Disenfranchised Grief --- Grief is disenfranchised when 1) the caregiver or 2) others do not recognize there is grief. The term is also appropriate when a person recognizes a loss but thinks it is not appropriate to grieve. The incorrect belief that grieving only happens after death is an example. Death caused by drug overdose is another.

DNR – Do Not Resuscitate. A directive or decision to not restart a heart or breathing.

End-of-Life Doula – a person who provides nonmedical comfort and support to a dying person and the family.

Family Caregiver – an individual who commits to taking care of a loved one who has a long-term disease. Most family caregivers are genetically connected and some others are psychologically connected.

Five Wishes – an easy-to-use advance directive form. It helps the family and authorities know what the loved one wishes. It can be used as a legal document directing chosen individuals to handle medical and comfort care, and to make funeral or memorial service arrangements. It is free and available online: **fivewishes.org**

Grief -- Grief is the way we adjust to significant loss. Adjustment can be easy and natural or difficult and heart-wrenching, depending on the strength of attachment to the person or thing lost.

Home-Care Assistance -- the provision of home services such as housekeeping, meal preparation, dressing, and bathing. AAA Community Living Services provides some funds for Home Care Assistance for seniors.

Home Health Care—the provision of health-related services at home that require a trained professional. Medicare often pays for covered people.

Hospice – Hospice provides late stage care at home or in a health care facility. The goal is to help patients live the last stage of their lives with comfort and dignity. A hospice contract requires the family to stop seeking curative procedures. Support is also provided to the family.

Meals on Wheels – a Federal program that provides meals to elderly and disabled people. The program is administered by local organizations through the AAA.

Medical Power of Attorney (MPOA), see also Power of Attorney – a legal document that assigns a trusted person the authority to make medical decisions on behalf of a person who is incompetent.

Memory Care Facility – a secure unit with professional caregivers who are trained to care for patients with dementia.

Mild Cognitive Impairment (MCI) – a mental dysfunction such as poor memory that does not affect the ability to live independently. It does not necessarily foretell a neurological disease.

PACE (Program for All-inclusive Care for the Elderly) -- a federally funded program available in 124 locations in several states. It is a health management program designed to enable caregivers to provide quality home care for the elderly.

Palliative Care -- a medical term for treatment of the whole person with a serious illness. It includes curative and comfort care (pain management, nursing, occupational therapy and counselling). All patients should have the best quality of life possible throughout their medical treatment.

Parkinson's disease -- a progressive disorder of the nervous system that affects movement. Tremors are common, but the disorder may also cause stiffness, slowing of movement, falling, difficulty with swallowing and dementia. For information search for the American Parkinson Disease Association's website: apdaparkinson.org

Power of Attorney (POA), see also Medical Power of Attorney – a legal document that assigns a trusted person the authority to make decisions concerning finances, property and personal and business assets on behalf of a person who is incompetent.

Respite – a time for the caregiver to have a break from the routine of caregiving. A loved one may be temporarily placed in a facility. Sometimes it means just taking a break to recuperate for a few minutes or hours.

Skilled Care -- the highest level of care provided in a nursing home. Doctors prescribe care that is provided by licensed health professionals, like nurses, physical therapists and occupational therapists.

Sundowning – a behavior associated with dementia in which a person becomes more confused and agitated in the late afternoon and evening. Wandering is also more likely.

Therapeutic Lie – a statement used to distract someone with dementia even if the statement may not true.

Validation – a technique to communicate and manage behaviors of people who have some form of dementia such as Alzheimer's.

The Authors

Glen A. Hinshaw

Glen grew up in Denver, Colorado and followed his dad exploring, fishing, and hunting in the wilderness areas of Colorado. He wanted to be a Colorado Wildlife Officer since he was a teenager. He pursued his dream and graduated from Colorado State University with a Bachelor of Science degree in Wildlife Management. He enjoyed a 34-year career with Colorado Parks and Wildlife and was Wildlife Officer for 25 years. For his last nine years he held several regional staff positions and retired as the Division's Education Coordinator for Western Colorado. All that experience as a wildlife manager didn't prepare him for the wild caregiver ride.

Life changed for Glen when his mother was diagnosed with Alzheimer's. After her death his wife was inflicted with the same dreaded disease. Altogether, he cared for them for 36 years. He was a long-distance caregiver as well as a home caregiver and was their advocate when he placed them into nursing homes.

Glen's counselor walked alongside him and helped him be a better caregiver. He attended caregiver workshops, seminars, conferences, and participated in support groups that gave him insight and greater ability to cope with being a caregiver. He put all that information and experience into his first book: *Caregiver: My Tempestuous Journey.*

Glen was a member of the AAA Community Living Advisory Council in his area, where he learned how to connect caregivers with local resources. After retirement he made himself available to share his caregiving knowledge and experience. He met Laird Landon and together they facilitate family caregiver support groups for no fee. Glen is a passionate peer-coach who listens with an empathy and compassion. He encourages other caregivers to start support groups if they don't yet have one in their area.

Other books by Glen Hinshaw:

"Caregiver: My Tempestuous Journey" is an autobiographical account of Glen's 36-year caregiving journey. Available from Amazon.com

"Echoes from the Mountains: The Life and Adventures of a Colorado Wildlife Officer" is Glen's autobiography about how a city boy followed his dream to be a Colorado Wildlife Officer and his 34-year career Available from Amazon.com

"Crusaders for Wildlife, 2nd Edition" is a 200-year history about the wildlife of Southwest Colorado. Follow me on Facebook at Glen A. Hinshaw-author

E. Laird Landon Jr.

Laird grew up in San Diego playing baseball and tennis as often as he could. He was crushed that he could not become Willie Mays or Rod Laver, so he went to college. He earned a BS with distinction from San Diego State College and PhD with distinction from UCLA. All diplomas were signed by Governor Ronald Reagan, none of which prepared him for his wife's dementia or for caregiving.

Laird was a professor of marketing and management at the University of California, Riverside; the University of Colorado, Boulder and the University of Houston. After President Reagan began a wave of banking deregulation, Laird consulted with banks to help them compete. He was a popular speaker to trade groups and helped with strategic planning, commercial bank marketing and management. He taught in every national banking school, and, for a short while, was the academic director of the American Bankers Association's Stonier School of Banking. After retiring he started and managed a registered financial advisory firm.

That was before his wife, Marilyn, was diagnosed with pseudo-bulbar palsy. Caring for his wife has been the most challenging, emotionally difficult and exhausting chapter of his life. It has also led to profound positive change, self-discovery, and a mission to help others manage and grow from caregiving. While a caregiver, he realized how deeply caregivers grieve. He was certified as a grief coach by the Creative Grief Studio and has been a volunteer grief counselor for a local mental health agency.

Laird facilitates caregiver support groups with Glen Hinshaw. He helps others organize support groups and coaches individual caregivers and grievers. He gives presentations about caregiving to family and professional caregivers.

Caregiving: Journey to a New Horizon You may order directly from us. Bulk orders can save on shipping costs. Retail booksellers can purchase books wholesale. Glen and Laird's passion is to help caregivers. We are available to speak at conferences, trade shows, seminars, professional associations, and other groups that support caregivers.
Available from Amazon in paperback or as a Kindle eBook.
On Facebook search for us: 'Caregiver Journey' or 'Caregiver Support'.
Email us: CaregiverSupport@icloud.com.

Made in the USA
San Bernardino, CA
16 June 2020